WITTGENSTEIN'S PHILOSOPHY OF MIND

WITTGENSTEIN'S PHILOSOPHY OF MIND

ASHOK VOHRA

OPEN COURT
La Salle, Illinois

OPEN COURT and the above logo are registered in the U.S. Patent and Trademark Office. Published by arrangement with Croom Helm Ltd., Beckenham, Kent.

© 1986 Ashok Vohra. All rights reserved. No part of this publication may be reproduced, stored in a retrieval system, or transmitted in any form or by any means, electronic, mechanical, photocopying, recording or otherwise, without the prior written permission of the publisher, Open Court Publishing Company, La Salle, Illinois 61301.

OC 903   10 9 8 7 6 5 4 3 2 1

Library of Congress Cataloging in Publication Data

Vohra, Ashok, 1949–
   Wittgenstein's philosophy of mind.

   Includes bibliographical references and index.
   1. Wittgenstein, Ludwig, 1889–1951—Contributions
in philosophy of mind. 2. Intellect—History—20th
century. I. Title.
B3376.W564V64   1986b   128'.2'0924   85-31983
ISBN 0-8126-9031-1

Printed and bound in Great Britain

CONTENTS

Preface

Introduction — 1

1. The Concept of Sensation — 9
2. Privacy and Private Language — 34
3. Self-Knowledge and Personal Identity — 68
4. Knowledge of Other Persons — 95

Concluding Note — 111

Index — 113

That which I am writing about so tediously, may be obvious to someone whose mind is less decrepit.'

Wittgenstein
Remarks on Colour.

To My Parents

PREFACE

Kierkegaard wrote 'Fixed ideas are like a cramp in your foot; the best remedy is to stamp on them.' Few thinkers in history have had the courage to do so. Wittgenstein was one of those who could not only break with the dominant academic tradition of his times, but also had the courage to reject the early ideas expounded by him in the *Tractatus Logico-Philosophicus*, and to propound radically different ones. Although the gnomic style of Wittgenstein has the distinct advantage of speaking directly to his readers, some people think that it has a rather corrosive effect in the sense that at the end of a reading of his ideas one is left with nothing positive. It is alleged that Wittgenstein has a destructive mind. In this book I have tried to dispel this misconception about him.

It is the object of this book to present a concise exposition of the later Wittgenstein's philosophy of mind. I believe that for a faithful exposition of a thought or a point of view it is necessary to appreciate it, and in order to appreciate a thought system it is essential to empathise with it. But it is not possible to have an empathy with a viewpoint unless one has also understood the complex concepts employed in it. It is with the sole intention of clarifying the usage of such concepts that I have, at times, in the course of this book, made reflective or critical comments. However, the present work is not intended to be an exhaustive account of Wittgenstein's philosophy of mind. I intend it to be only an analytic study of its foundations. Whatever originality this book possesses derives almost entirely from the insights found in the writings of Wittgenstein. In writing this book I have avoided confusing profundity with obscurity. I have employed a clear and simple conceptual apparatus, to present my point of view. How far I have succeeded in this is for others to judge.

The present work is a revised version of my thesis which I submitted to the University of Delhi for the award of PhD degree. In its earlier form it was read and commented upon by Professors H.D. Lewis, K.J. Shah, Margaret Chatterjee, Mrinal Miri, Rajendra Prasad and R.C. Pandeya. It is a pleasure to be able to acknowledge their help. I have made some changes in the light of some of their comments. For the faults and shortcomings of this book, however, I alone am responsible.

I sincerely thank my wife Asha for undertaking the arduous task of correcting the typed script and suggesting some stylistic changes.

It would be ungrateful on my part if I did not express my gratitude to my sister Sushma who always provided me with emotional support at the times when I needed it most.

Last but not least, I am thankful to Dr Stuart Shanker and Mr Richard Stoneman for their interest in the publication of the manuscript.

AV
St Stephen's College, Delhi

INTRODUCTION

Though a distinction was drawn between mind and matter as early as Plato and St Augustine, Descartes was the first philosopher to state the distinction between the two clearly. He held mind to be diametrically opposite to matter. While matter for him was all public physical existents like rocks, chairs, tables, and so on, mind for him was a non-physical substance whose essential nature is thinking, and by it he meant something that differentiates a person from other things. Persons are different from other things like rocks and chairs, and mind is that which names the difference. It was held by Descartes that mind is a private entity and all the mental acts, such as thinking, believing, meaning and understanding, are private processes. They are private to each individual because, it is held, they are directly accessible only to the respective bearers. This view gives rise to the following problem:

In our day-to-day life we communicate our thoughts, feelings, intentions, and other mental acts, or psychical processes, to each other by speaking or writing. Speaking and writing are physical processes that take place in the external, public world; but the mental processes which they express are private. This asymmetry between language and mental processes gives rise to the following questions:

(a) What are the connections of speech with language on the one hand, and with mental processes or acts on the other?
(b) How do words refer to different mental acts?
(c) How is it that different people mean the same things by the common mental act vocabulary?

Descartes says nothing explicitly about any of these problems; but his conception of the possible answers to them was, understandably, the one that dominated British empiricism. It is held by all these philosophers, namely Descartes, Locke, Berkeley and Hume, that the immediate objects of awareness of mind are its ideas. Now, if this were so, then certain consequences regarding the relation between language, and mental contents like thoughts, feelings, and sensations that it conveys would follow. On this view, words are the marks of the ideas in the mind of the speaker, and language stands in purely an external relation to thinking. This conception of language does not only imply that thinking could be without language but it also implies that a person could have, or in principle invent, a private language to record his own experiences, feelings and thoughts for his exclusive use. It seemed to these philosophers that mental concepts, or mental contents vocabulary are learned as a matter of course; that we learn them from introspection by giving ourselves a 'private ostensive definition'. This definition is ostensive, because in it instead of physically pointing to the object we mentally fix our attention on the inner process and make a connection between it (the process) and the word. It is private, because it takes place in each one's mind, such that no one else can be aware of what is going on in that mind.

This conception of language gives rise to a further problem: If each one of us learned the mental concepts from our own case, then we need some solid justification for the conviction that the same processes occur in minds other than our own; or in other words we would need a foundation for our belief that besides mine there are other minds also. Our knowledge of other minds, on this type of theory, was naturally based on analogy. For the reasons mentioned in Chapter Four,[1] the argument from analogy turns topsy-turvy. To my mind these philosophers thus failed to give any satisfactory answer to any of the problems which were the consequences of their theories.

Philosophers who do not accept dualism hold that mind and matter are one. In other words, these philosophers fall into materialistic monism. The most cogent and plausible form of monism is logical, or methodological behaviourism. It would be appropriate here to draw a distinction between metaphysical behaviourism on the one hand and logical, or methodological behaviourism on the other hand. While metaphysical behaviourism denies the existence of psychical occurrences, methodological behaviourism leaves open the question of the existence of mental processes and when it holds that psychical occurrences exist, it restricts itself to supplying behavioural criteria for all that is mental. It believes that psychology should in common with the established sciences deal exclusively with intersubjectively observable phenomena and not rely on non-intersubjectively confirmable reports of occurrences in the minds of its subjects. Logical behaviourism, also sometimes called analytic behaviourism, holds that the psychological statements, whether they are about other minds or about one's own mind, are translatable into statements about physical occurrences or physical states. In logical or analytic behaviourism the viewpoint is one not of science but of logical or conceptual analysis. It says that the meaning of mental statements is analysable, without remainder, into statements about behaviour and about the observable circumstances in which such behaviour occurred. Gilbert Ryle is an exponent of logical behaviourism. Though logical behaviourism is capable of giving satisfactory answers to some of the problems which the mental theorists faced, it is mistaken in many respects. The following are two major objections against behaviourism:

(a) Logical behaviourists held that one makes ascriptions of mental states to oneself in much the same way as one ascribes them to others. But this is wrong, for it is a basic feature of mental concepts that there is radical asymmetry between their application by oneself to oneself and their application by oneself to others. Mental concepts are applied by us to other persons on the basis of some observable change or continuance, or some other similar aspect of their physical state. But we do not apply them to ourselves on this basis. Thus, a behaviourist, who fails to see this asymmetry, gives an incorrect account of the use of mental concepts.

(b) Logical behaviourism holds that mental descriptions are equivalent to purely physical descriptions. But this seems odd; because one cannot, for the most part, give physical descriptions of each and every mental act, say, for example, of happiness, or thinking. Even if such descriptions could be given, the listener would surely not understand them, however descriptive these descriptions may claimed to be.

Some readers of Wittgenstein allege that he advocates an extreme form of philosophical behaviourism. For example, J.J.C. Smart in 'Materialism' says: 'in spite of his own disclaimer, Wittgenstein is in fact a sort of behaviourist'.[2] But this seems to me for the following reasons to be a misinterpretation of Wittgenstein:[3]

(i) Wittgenstein does not always employ criteria of the behavioural type alone. For him, it is the other circumstances, the total situation at the moment, the knowledge gained and the competence acquired in the past, and the like that are equally important. For example, whether someone has understood subtraction or addition is determined not only by what he does, but also whether he has learned a routine for operating with series, whether he is a good mathematician, and a host of other factors unanalysable behaviouristically.

(ii) Even when Wittgenstein refers to actual behaviour, it is never the present short-term behaviour that serves as a criterion. He refers not only to the past but also to the future behaviour. For example, to say that someone has understood subtraction or addition is not to say that he can do it at the time t, but it means that he can do it on future occasions also.

(iii) While behaviourism supplies the behavioural criterion for the truth and falsity of psychological statements, it does not explicate the sense of everyday expressions that relate to the understanding of words such as 'mean' and 'understand'. Wittgenstein throughout insists on making the sense of these words clear.

(iv) Behaviourism tries to capture by means of behavioural criteria alone the nature of understanding, or, in general, all the mental acts. Thus, to a behaviourist, the question 'What does understanding, or fixing one's attention, or meaning consist in?' makes a sensible question. To Wittgenstein, it does not. He considers all such questions senseless and rejects them.

In the present work, I have tried to bring out Wittgenstein's intentions clearly. Besides this, I have tried to give a positive account of his philosophy of mind. It is original in this respect. For it is generally said even by readers well versed in Philosophy that Wittgenstein's thought is incomprehensible and obscure because it is 'too complex' and it is generally held by the readers of Wittgenstein that he has a destructive mind, because it is alleged that at the end of a study of his writings there is the impression of being left with nothing positive. In this study, I have shown that this impression is false. In the course of arriving at his positive philosophy of mind, I have answered the major problems that were faced by both the Cartesian theorists and the logical behaviourists.

To my mind, in philosophy, problems arise because of an excessive tendency on the part of philosophers to theorise about even the simplest of human experiences. The problem of mind, especially as it has been raised and discussed by René Descartes and the whole generation of his followers, is one of the living examples of this tendency. In the present study, I have tried to develop an argument to show, quite contrary to the popular, and indeed influential, philosophical opinion, that there is no epistemological problem of mind whatever, and that the widespread philosophical scepticism with respect to our knowledge of minds has no foundation at all. As a heuristic principle for developing my argument, I have throughout followed what one might call a Wittgensteinian dictum *of placing everything as it is undistorted before us* — to create complete clarity which leads to the complete disappearance of the philosophical problems.

In the first chapter, I analyse the concept of sensation. This analysis is important; for, philosophers, especially the Cartesian theorists, have a tendency to use 'sensation', 'sense-data', and 'sensible qualities' interchangeably. After this analysis, I seek to answer the question 'What are the immediate objects of observation?' The scrutiny of the various answers given to it by philosophers, especially the theorists, is necessary, because those philosophers who hold that the mind is a theatre, or an agent, and that the mental occurrences/events are private are led to think that the immediate objects of observation must be either sensible qualities, sensations, or sense-data. I try to show that the immediate objects of observations are neither sensible qualities, nor sensations, nor sense-data but the objects as they are in the public physical world. In arriving at this thesis I have examined critically the major theories which support the view that the immediate objects of observation are either sensible qualities, or sensations, or sense-data, and have shown the logical absurdities involved in the view.

Having established in the first chapter that we need not posit private entities such as sensations, sense impressions, or sense-data to account for observation, I try to show in the second chapter that the individual needs no private, or special language to register his thoughts, feelings, or sensations. For, we can and in fact we always do register our sensations in the ordinary (public) language. In arriving at this conclusion, I have examined and exposed, (a) the error about the nature of experience, and (b) the error about the nature of language, which underlie the mistaken view that we need a private language to register our thoughts, feelings, and sensations. I have supported Wittgenstein's view that the relation between words and psychical phenomena is not contingent but essential, and that language is not the product of one person, but has evolved with human life. This view has had a revolutionary effect in the history of the philosophy of mind. For, if there is no private language, then there are no special problems of self-knowledge, and knowledge of other minds. I have maintained the thesis that the concept of 'private language' rests on a category mistake. This thesis forms the nucleus of the present work.

In the third chapter, I utilise the conclusions of the first two chapters — viz. sensations are neither private (first chapter), nor do we need a private language to express them (second chapter) — to show that self-knowledge, or the knowledge of one's own mind is attained neither by introspection, nor through any other 'method' to which the owner has a privileged access, but that it is gained by and through the knowledge of the world, or the total *form of life*. In this respect I have sharply departed from Gilbert Ryle's view that one knows about one's own self in much the same way in which one knows about other minds. To establish my thesis that a person does not use any theory to know about his own mind, I have done two things: I have further examined and rejected some of the major theories about the nature of mind, and the connected 'introspection theory' of self-knowledge; and secondly I have discussed the nature of personal identity. In the main, I have criticised the theories advocating the memory or bodily criteria of personal identity. I have argued for the thesis that we need not have any special theories to account for the first person identity judgement. I have shown that one who considers that self-knowledge and personal identity present a problem is mistaken; for, he fails to recognise that it is a basic feature of our life that we know about ourselves and about our identity without any theories whatever.

In the fourth chapter, I try to show that there is no special epistemic problem about the knowledge of other minds or the identity of other persons. For, it is the basic feature of our life that we know that the other walking and talking figures having human shape and form that we see and hear do have minds. To support this thesis I have done two things. 1. I discussed the basic assumptions that give rise to the problem of other minds, and also critically examined the various arguments offered by the theorists to account for the knowledge of other minds. 2. I have argued for the thesis that the third person identity judgements are based on the behavioural criteria, including the similarity of the bodily appearance. To establish my thesis I have critically scrutinised the various objections to the view which regards bodily identity as a criterion for asserting third person identity judgements. Here I have discussed and replied to the change-of-body argument put forward by Shoemaker.

My thesis is that mind is neither private nor any kind of substantival entity which is observable by its possessor alone and no one else, but that it is observable to anybody through behaviour,[4] including linguistic behaviour, together with the contextual complex in which such behaviour occurs. This thesis is the outcome of my examination of both the mental theorists and the logical behaviourist theories, particularly Ryle's. In developing it, I have carefully avoided skepticism and agreed with Wittgenstein. One of its interesting aspects is that the science of psychology presupposes this thesis, though it is open to the psychologist to adopt any method convenient to him, and suitable for his purposes to organise knowledge about minds.

In this study I have not considered a more prudent theory, namely, the mind-brain identity theory. According to this theory, mental processes are in reality the processes in the brain. These processes have been called neurophysiological processes. On this view to have an experience X is for one's brain to be in a state Y, in the way in which lightning is an electric discharge, or temperature is the mean kinetic energy of molecules. The identity between the mental experiences and brain processes is not an equivalence of concepts, which could be discovered *a priori*, but something which is established on the basis of empirical research. My reasons for not considering this theory are:

(i) The methodology adopted by the supporters of mind-brain identity theory is scientific, whereas the methodology adopted in the present study is the logical analysis of ordinary language in which mental phenomena are described.

(ii) When the physiologist tries to describe some mental phenomenon, say, joking, in terms of some physio-chemical changes in the brain cells, his description forms no part of the ordinary description of joking. He tells us an altogether different story. He does not tell us about the art and craft of joking, but of some scientific process involved in joking. Moreover, the capacity of a person to make a joke, or to do any mental act, is not due to some physio-chemical changes in the brain cells but due to the sense of humour of that person. How can a child be taught the art and craft of making a joke by telling him about the brain process involved in joking!

(iii) Even if mental acts could be accounted for in terms of neurophysiological changes in brain cells, our speech habits would not change. It is one thing to talk about the mental acts and quite another to talk about the physiology of brain — as, for example, it is one thing to talk about seeing and quite another to talk about the physiology of perception.

Notes

1. See pp. 95-110.
2. In *The Mind-Brain Identity Theory*, ed. C.V. Borst, London: Macmillan, 1970, pp. 159-70.
3. For an excellent discussion on the question whether Wittgenstein is a behaviourist see Wolfgang Stegmüller, *Main Currents in Contemporary German, British and American Philosophy*, Holland: D. Reidel Publishing Company, 1969, pp. 481-3.
4. The term 'behaviour' is used here to refer to not only the present behaviour but also the future and past behaviour.

1 THE CONCEPT OF SENSATION

In this chapter, I analyse the concept of sensation. This analysis is important, for philosophers, especially the Cartesian theorists, have a tendency to use 'sensations', 'sense-data', and 'sensible qualities' interchangeably. After this analysis, I seek to answer the question 'What are the immediate objects of observation?' The scrutiny of the various answers given to it by philosophers, especially the theorists, is necessary, because those philosophers who hold that the mind is a theatre, or an agent, and mental occurrences/events are private are led to think that the immediate objects of observation must be either sensible qualities, or sensations, or sense-data. I try to show that the immediate objects of observation are neither sensible qualities, nor sensations, nor sense-data, but the objects as they are in the public physical world.

A sensation is that which a normal human being naturally has when his body stands in a certain kind of relationship to different kinds of physical objects or different kinds of surroundings. For example, if a human being is made to stand before a furnace for a long time, he starts having an uncomfortable feeling, namely, a sensation of burning. The *Oxford English Dictionary* describes 'sensation' as an operation of any of the senses; a psychical affection or state of consciousness consequent on and related to a particular impression received by one of the bodily organs, or a particular impression required by one of the organs of sense. Based on this description we can draw a distinction between two types of sensation:

(a) those which are connected with special organs of sense, namely, eyes, ears, nose, tongue and skin;
(b) those which are connected with other sensitive but non-sensory parts of the body.

The latter are generally called organic sensations. Pains, aches, tickles, prickings, fatigue and giddiness, fall under this latter category (b). Seeing, hearing, tasting, smelling and feeling come under the former category (a), namely, the sensations connected with special organs of sense. However, the distinction between the two is quite arbitrary because both can, and in fact are, used interchangeably. For example, when our eyes are dazzled, or we have a fish-bone in the throat, or we are pricked in the skin, we readily say that we have pain. Conversely, whenever we have an organic sensation, for example, pain in the throat or stomach, or we are fatigued, we are apt to say that we feel the fish bone in the throat, or suet pudding in the stomach, or the resistance of a log. However, the main point of distinction is that while it is proper to ask for the cause of organic sensations, that is, pain, ache, fatigue, and so on, there is no sense in asking for the cause of the sensations connected with our special organs of sense. For example, in our day-to-day life, we do talk of causes of pain, causes of fatigue, causes of tickling, but we never ask the question, 'What is the cause of seeing, or tasting, or smelling, or feeling, or hearing?' In fact this question is analogous to the question: 'What is the cause of writing the word "Delhi" as it is written? Nobody asks such questions. This question obviously makes no sense. As the question about seeing, hearing, tasting, smelling, and feeling is analogous to it, therefore, that question also makes no sense. Generally, the cause of an organic sensation can be a sensation connected with our special sense organs. For example, to the questions 'What is the cause of the pain in the throat?' or 'What is the cause of fatigue?', one is justified in replying that the fish bone in the throat is the cause of the pain in the throat, or that the pressure of a log on the body is the cause of fatigue, or that the cooked beans that one ate the previous night is the cause of the stomach ache.

One of the difficulties faced in discussing the logic of the concept of sensation of seeing, hearing, tasting, smelling and feeling is linguistic in nature. The linguistic difficulty arises because of the fact that we do not talk in terms of 'neat' sensation vocabulary.[1] We do not just talk of seeing, hearing, tasting, smelling, or feeling alone; but we talk of seeing something (say, haystacks), hearing something (say, the approach of an engine), tasting something (say, apples), smelling something (say, roses), feeling something (say, hot or cold). 'We ordinarily mention them only in reference to the things or events which we are observing or trying to observe or claiming to observe'.[2] In fact, we describe our sensations by referring to how common objects regularly look, feel, or sound to any normal human being. For example, when I hear the approach of an engine, I am apt to describe this sensation as a humming thing, or when asked to describe a sensation of taste to someone I readily say that it tastes like sugar. This method of describing our sensations in impersonal or neutral terms is of great theoretical importance for our communication. They are the terms which anybody can in' principle observe. We expect that their accounts of such descriptions would tally, or at least are capable of correction until they tally. If we had not couched the description of our sensations in these neutral or impersonal terms, then they would fail to convey anything. 'These are, after all, the terms which we learned by being taught them by others. We do not and cannot describe haystacks in terms of this or that set of sensations. We describe our sensations by certain sorts of references to observers and things like haystacks.'[3]

This holds good in the case of organic sensations too. We do not merely talk of pains, aches and itches, but we describe, for instance, our sensation of pain as stabbing, grinding, or burning pain. By this we do not mean that the pain is necessarily invoked by a knife, or a drill, or a burning rod; rather we mean that our pain is like the pain which is caused to anybody by such instruments.

Confusion regarding the use of 'sensation' arises because many philosophers tend to use words like 'pain', 'itch' and 'ache', as 'neat' sensation names. They forget that 'sensations' has a complicated use. It is used to refer to three different kinds of entities, namely, (a) an act of awareness, or sensory experience, as, for example, pain, or aching; (b) the entity of which one is aware, or the content of sensory experience, as, for example, aches and pains; and (c) sometimes, it is employed as a comprehensive term to refer to both (a) and (b). Confusion arises because it is frequently used without qualifications as to whether an act of sensation (i.e., sensing) is meant, or the content of sensation (i.e., what is sensed) is meant; or a complex of both act and content is meant. In short, the confusion arises because of the mistake of assimilation of the concept of 'observing', that is the act of awareness, to the concept of 'sensation', that is, the content of awareness. In what follows, I shall try to draw a conceptual distinction between 'sensation' and 'observation'.

We say that a person is observing something if he is trying with or without success to find out something about it by doing at least some looking, scanning, listening, smelling, savouring, or feeling.

Observing something necessarily implies the having of at least one of the visual, auditory, gustatory, olfactory, or any other sensation. There is a contradiction, a kind of logical oddity, involved in saying that someone was looking or peeping, at something without having a single glimpse of it, or that someone was listening to something without having even a single auditory sensation. 'Having at least one sensation is part of the force of "perceiving", "overhearing", "savouring" and the rest'.[4] But the converse does not hold good. Having a sensation alone cannot itself be a species of perceiving, hearing, or savouring any more than bricks are houses, or alphabets are words. Observing something entails not only having a sensation but also paying heed to it. In the form of a formula we can say:

Observation = Having a sensation + Paying heed to it.

Furthermore, we can say a number of things about 'observation' which we cannot say about 'sensation'. Firstly, observing is a task which one can perform methodically or haphazardly, accurately or inaccurately, carefully, or carelessly, expertly or amateurishly. One can be good or bad at doing it. One can be more or less successful in it. But one cannot exercise all these 'powers of observation' in the case of sensations. One cannot have sensations systematically. For example, one can listen carefully, but one cannot have singing in the ears carefully. Secondly, we observe on purpose (for example, to find out what is happening around us), but we cannot have sensations on purpose. Thirdly, we can make mistakes in our observations but it makes no sense to talk of mistakes in sensations. Sensations cannot be correct or incorrect, veridical or non-veridical. In other words, they are 'mistake-proof'. 'But the reason why sensation cannot be mistaken is not because it is a mistake-proof observing, but because it is not an observing at all. It is as absurd to call a sensation veridical as to call it "mistaken". The senses are neither honest nor deceitful'.[5] Fourthly, by observing we mean finding out, or trying to find out something; but having a sensation is neither finding out nor failing to find out anything. In other words, observation is necessarily motivational while sensation is not. Fifthly, observing is a mental characteristic. It reflects on the intellect of a person. If a person quickly observes things correctly, we call him intelligent. On the other hand, sensations have nothing 'mental' about them. Having a sensation or not having a sensation does not reflect on the intellect of a person. For example, deafness is not a species of stupidity, nor is blindness thought of as a mental defect, nor is the attraction for a particular scent a sign of intelligence. In fact, we readily concede that both men and reptiles may have the same sorts of sensation when placed before a furnace, or when kept in a pond of ice; in short, when they live under the same conditions.

Another difficulty in discussing the logic of the concept of sensation is the tendency in philosophers to assimilate the concept of sensation to sense impressions and/or to the sensible qualities of things. Prominent among those who assimilate sensations to sensible qualities of objects is Berkeley. By sensible qualities are meant such qualities as colour, shape, size, motion, hardness, heat, sound, taste, and smell, in short, the qualities which are said to be perceived by our special sense organs. This assimilation of sensations to sensible qualities, is, however, not justified, because there are a number of things that can be said about the former but not about the latter, and vice versa. Firstly, we say that we see colours, shapes, sizes, motions, spatial relations of things, as, for example, side-by-sideness, above and below; we taste the tastes of things, smell their smells, hear the sounds emitted by them, touch hot things, and so on. In general, we say that we perceive the qualities of things. But, in the case of sensations, we do not say that we perceive sensations; rather we say that we have them or that we feel them.[6] Secondly, sensible qualities of objects continue to remain even if there is no person to perceive them. For example, the colour or the shape, or the spatial relations, or the emitted sounds, or the smells continue to be even if there is no perceiver. For, there is no contradiction involved in saying that there is/was a sensible quality (colour, shape, size, etc.) of which nobody is/was aware. That sensible qualities can exist unperceived is supported by the fact that in science whenever a new element, for instance, Ruthenium, is found, or a new property of an element, for instance, radioactivity, is found, it is called a discovery and not an invention. The grammar of the word 'discover' is such that we use it only in those cases in which we reveal certain qualities, which, though existent, were hitherto unknown. But, in the case of sensations, a contradiction is involved in saying that there was a sensation though nobody felt it. Sensations cannot exist unfelt or unhad. The *esse* of sensations is *sentri*. This is to say that sensations can exist only if they are felt or had by someone. We may or may not pay attention to our sensations if they are mild; but we cannot dispense with having them altogether. If we do not feel the pain at all, we certainly are not in pain.

Thirdly, the sensible qualities of physical objects can be perceived by anybody who is suitably placed and whose sense organs are in normal condition. For instance, the blue colour of the table top before me, now, can be seen by anyone who sees it and who is not colour blind. Similar is the case with size, shape, spatial relationships, and other sense-qualities of physical objects. But in the case of sensations, I alone can feel my sensations. Nobody, however competent or well placed he may be, can feel my sensations. In short, everybody in principle can perceive the sensible qualities of a physical object; but nobody except myself can feel my sensations.

Fourthly, in the case of sensible qualities there are chances of misperception. One may mistake, for example, a pink colour for a red colour, or an elliptical shape for a circular shape, or a pair of parallel lines for a pair of convergent lines. That is why it makes sense to say, 'It seems red to me', or 'It seems circular to me', or 'It seems a pair of convergent lines to me', or 'The water seems warm', or 'I seem to have fever.' But in the case of sensations, misperception is impossible. Talk of mistake in their context is out of place. That is why it is absurd to say 'I seem to have a pain.' One may be mistaken about the cause of pain but one cannot be mistaken about one's having a pain. From this, it follows that sensations cannot be identified with sensible qualities.

Let us now consider the question 'Are sensations identical with sense impressions, or what Berkeley calls ideas, or what has been called "sense-data" by later philosophers like Price, Moore and Russell?' By the terms 'sense impression', 'idea' and 'sense-datum', we mean what is present in our visual, auditory, gustatory, olfactory, or kinaesthetic field. For example, when an object looks blue to me, a psychologist is apt to say that there is something blue present in my visual field. A philosopher, at the same time, says that I am having a 'sense impression' or an 'idea', or 'sense-datum' of a blue colour. The following similarities in sensations and sense impressions have led philosophers to conclude that they are identical:

(a) About both sensations and sense impressions we say that we have them. We never say that we perceive them.

(b) We cannot be mistaken about both. If I say at a time t that I have a sense impression of blue, then I cannot be mistaken about the fact that the object in question seems blue to me at that particular time, t.
(c) As with sensations, I alone can have sense impressions. Nobody, however well placed he may be, can have the sense impressions of blue which I am having right now.
(d) Like sensations, sense impressions cannot exist unhad. If there are sense impressions, then somebody must have them.

Though there are these similarities between sensations and sense impressions, yet the two cannot be identified. For, if we do so, then we can talk about them indifferently, or synonymously and thus use the two expressions 'sensations' and 'sense impressions' interchangeably. We can speak, for example, about sensation of pain, sensation of colour, sensation of heat, sensation of extension, and also sense impression of pain, sense impression of colour, sense impression of extension, or sense impression of heat, without loss of meaning. But, to do so is really absurd. For, though trivially, the idiom 'sensation of ...' seems unnatural in the case of colour and extension. We do not use this idiom ordinarily for colour and extension. Conversely, though there are a few cases, for example, in the case of heat, where we can use sensation of heat and sense impression of heat interchangeably, yet there are a number of cases, pain being one of them, in which we cannot use the two expressions interchangeably. For example, to say 'sense impression of pain' seems odd and out of place, whereas 'sensation of pain' seems natural and in place.

Again, our sense impressions reflect or fail to reflect the nature of physical reality. For example, there is no distinction between 'looks blue' and 'is blue', 'feels hot' and 'is hot', 'looks extended' and 'is extended'. The physical reality determines the nature of the sense impression that we are going to have. We cannot have the sense impressions of qualities which are not present in the physical world. Pure air, for example, which is odourless and colourless, cannot produce in any observer the sense impression of a colour or odour. And *vice versa,* whenever a large number of normal observers do not have the sense impressions of smell or taste and so on, we conclude that the object under consideration does not possess the properties of taste and smell. We classify it as tasteless and odourless. But our sensations, though having a physical cause, do not reflect or fail to reflect the nature of physical reality.

With these clarifications in mind, we are now in a position to consider various answers to the question 'What are the immediate objects of perception?' Before attempting to answer this question, let us first try to elucidate a distinction between mediate and immediate objects of perception. In order to be able to do this clearly let us take the case of visual perception. Accordingly, we shall elucidate the distinction between 'mediate' and 'immediate' perception. According to Berkeley, we have immediate perception if no element of inference is involved. For example, when we hear an engine, the sound is the immediate object of perception, because in receiving it no inference is involved. But, when we hear an engine we have only a mediate perception, because we infer it from the sound, which is immediately heard, to the engine which is not immediately perceived. Thus, immediate objects of perception or observation are those which do not involve an element of inference at all. Mediate objects of observation, on the other hand, are those which involve an element of inference.

Secondly, we must try to see the importance of this question in philosophy. A satisfactory answer to this question is crucial for any philosopher. For, if he holds that what one observes are sensations, sense impressions, or sense-data, then though it is possible for two persons to have the same experience (for example, they can perceive the same object, hear the same sound, feel the same feeling), yet they do not sense (have) the same sensations, or sense-data; the sense-data which they respectively sense may be qualitatively similar but they cannot be numerically the same. And if one asks the philosophers who hold that one observes sense-data, sense impressions, or sensations, why two people cannot have the same sense-data, their answer is that sense-data are made private by definition. Historically, sense-data have been characterised in such a way that the statement that one person has another's sensation describes no possible situation.

So, on this account the experiences of each and every individual may be quite different. This account would entail various other problems, such as the problem of other minds, the problem of private language, scepticism, and the like. It is in this light that we want to know what, after all, are the objects of immediate perception.

We shall now consider the various answers given to this question.

A. Some philosophers and psychologists have answered this question by saying that what we immediately perceive are sensations. But this is absurd, because sensations are not the sort of thing that can be perceived or observed. The following argument supports this thesis:

We have already shown that observing something entails having, at least, one sensation. For example, when someone is said to be observing a football match, it is implied that he is having at least one glimpse of it. If sensations were the proper objects of observation, then observing them must entail having at least one glimpse of those sensations, or at least one sensation of those sensations. But this is absurd, because football matches are just the sort of thing that we do get glimpses of, and sensations are not the sort of thing of which it is proper to say that we have glimpses. Moreover, if it is held that glimpses are the proper objects of observation, then observing them must entail having a glimpse of the glimpse. But this is absurd, as there is nothing answering to the phrase 'glimpse of a glimpse' or 'sensation of a sensation'. Even if there were something to correspond to them, the series would go on *ad infinitum.*

Secondly, when somebody has been observing something — say, watching a horse race — it is proper to ask him whether his observation was careless or careful, or whether he tried to see of it as much as he could, and other similar questions. If sensations were the proper objects of observation, then it would be proper to ask these questions: 'Is your tickle close or casual?' or 'Could you discern more about it?' or 'Is your tickle hampered or unhampered?' But nobody asks these questions any more than anyone asks 'How are the alphabets spelled?' No such questions can possibly be raised about sensations.

Thirdly, whatever we observe has shape, size, position, temperature, colour, smell, and many other sense qualities. Sensations have none of them. Though all of us agree that sensations do not have temperature, or colour, or smell, yet some of us may object and say that sensations do have location or position, in the sense that when confronted with the question 'Where is?' we may reply 'In my foot' in the case of a tickle, or 'In my nose' in the case of stinging. But all of us agree that this is a different sense of 'in'; the word 'in' is not used in a locative sense, that is to say; 'in' in all these answers is not used in the same sense in which it is used in 'bones are in my foot' or 'nostrils are in my nose'.

18 The Concept of Sensation

Finally, we can say with Ryle:

> it is perfectly clear that usually when I see, hear, taste, or smell anything, or detect something by touch, I do not suffer from any discomfort or pain in my eyes, ears, tongue, nose or finger tips. Seeing a tree does not hurt my eyes; and hearing a bird singing does not set up the slightest sort of tickling feeling in my ears. Sometimes, certainly, looking at things, like the head lights of motor cars, or listening to things, like the whistle of railway engine a few yards away, does hurt my eyes and ears. But not only is this exceptional but still more important, these disagreeable sensations do not help, they hinder perception. I see much better when I am not being dazzled than when I am. Sensations, in this sense, are not usually present when perception occurs; and when they are present they tend to impair perception. They are not *sine qua nons* of perception.[7]

It follows from the above arguments and considerations that sensations are not the sort of thing that can be observed. However, by saying this, we do not mean that they are unobservable in the way in which infra-microscopic bacteria, flying bullets, or atoms are unobservable; nor that they are unobservable to the blind. That is, we do not mean that the task of observing our sensations is one of insuperable difficulty. Or that we do not have a sense organ to observe them. By calling sensations unobservable we mean that sensations belong to the category to which neither the concept observable nor the concept of unobservable can be applied. This can be elucidated by taking the example of an alphabet. All of us know that words have spellings, but if someone asked us 'What is the spelling of an alphabet?' we would certainly be right in saying that this is an improper question. The question of spelling is not askable in the context of an alphabet. Similarly, the question of observation cannot be asked in the case of sensations.

B. The other answer to the question 'What are the immediate objects of perception?' is that the immediate objects of observation, or perception are sense-data, or sense impressions. The supporters of this theory are known as sense-datum philosophers and the theory is called sense-datum theory.[8] Before considering the sense-datum theory let us, first of all, be clear about the characteristics of sense-data. Though there are a number of disagreements amongst the various supporters of this theory, yet there are a number of characteristics of sense-data on which they all agree. These are:

(i) 'Sense-data' refers to what is given in immediate sense-experience.

(ii) 'Sense-data' are ontologically distinct from physical objects, or even from surfaces of physical objects. By physical objects is meant something that has extension, and whose existence does not depend upon its being perceived by anybody.

(iii) The *esse* of sense-data is *percepi*. Each one of the sense-data is private to the individual who has or experiences it.

We shall now examine the sense-datum theory.

David Hume, precursor of modern empiricism, held that 'all the perceptions of human mind resolve themselves into two distinct kinds, which I shall call IMPRESSIONS and IDEAS'.[9] He adds that impressions are more forceful and lively than ideas. They are what we are directly aware of in ordinary sense perception. Hume thinks it to be obvious that, whenever we use our senses, we are presented with sense-data. He does not give any proof for this, and takes it for granted. But, nothing can be more wrong-headed than this, because everybody (including sense-datum philosophers) believes that when we use our senses we are confronted with physical things and events in the physical world; we definitely do not think that we are confronted with something else, namely, sense-data. We all know that sense impressions or sense-data are not discovered or known in the way in which we come to know pains and tickles, or in the way in which we come to know that we sometimes detect by sight, hearing, taste, and touch.[10] Sense-data, at the most, remain theoretical entities, and the states of awareness of them are theoretical states, posited by a few philosophers to explain the phenomena of illusion and perception; they are not what everyone must recognise to be observable.

There is another group of philosophers, prominent among them being B. Russell, A.J. Ayer, H.H. Price, who agree in that sense-data, like magnetic fields, or electric currents, are theoretical entities, existence of which has to be argued for. They offer various deductive proofs for the 'existence' of sense-data. These proofs can be classified under the following heads:

(i) Argument from illusion or hallucinations.
(ii) Argument from verification or the argument from differential certainty.

(iii) Argument from causation.

The first two arguments for the existence of sense-data, given by Ayer,[11] Price,[12] and Russell[13] depend on the definition of a physical object. A physical object is usually defined in such a way that it cannot exist in a dream. From this definition, it follows that the object existing in one's dream is not physical. On this definition, if a book is a physical object, then it follows that one cannot assert that it exists simply on the ground that it can be perceived; for one's perception may be delusive. There are two ways to free ourselves from this difficulty; one is to allow the existence of physical objects even in our dreams. The other is to introduce a non-physical object, namely, a set of sense-data, which is allowed to exist in both veridical as well as delusive perception. The first alternative is not accepted by the sense-datum philosophers because it tends to demolish the distinction between delusive and veridical perceptions; they are led, therefore, to adopt the second alternative. It is in this sense that Price is successful in doubting the existence of a tomato but not that of the red patch of colour.[14] The doubt in the former case is possible, because tomato being a physical object is not allowed to enter in one's dream whereas a red patch of colour being a sense-datum is allowed to enter into a dream. One cannot, therefore, raise the possibility of a dream to doubt the red patch of colour whereas one can raise such a possibility in the case of tomato. Similarly, on Ayer's view also veridical and delusive perceptions should not be applicable to 'sense-data' which are not physical.[15]

The general line of argument in all these proofs is as follows: they start with the existence of a certain perceptual phenomenon or a perceptual fact, and with that they try to show that this phenomenon or fact entails the existence of sense-data. We shall now state and examine these arguments one by one.

The Argument from Illusion or Hallucination

This argument in its most general and comprehensive form is based on the fact that material things appear differently to different observers or the same observer in different conditions. The nature of these appearances depends upon the condition of the observers, a stick, for example, normally looks straight, but it looks bent when seen through water, and a plate which looks circular from one point of view may look elliptical from another point of view, and to people under the influence of drugs — say, LSD, or marijuana — things appear to change their colours. The cases of double vision, mirage, and twinkling of the stars present other familiar examples. This is not peculiar to visual appearances only, but applies as well to the domain of all other senses too. For example, the taste of things changes according to the palate, or a liquid seems to have different temperatures, according as to whether the hand that is feeling it is itself hot or cold; though in reality things do not change their shape, size, smell, or taste. A stick, for example, looks bent when immersed in water; but in fact it remains straight. So, what we see when it looks bent is not the quality of the stick. But, our experience of seeing it bent is not an experience of nothing; it has a definite content. Accordingly, it is said that we experience 'sense-data' which are similar to what we would be experiencing if we were seeing a real bent stick. From this, it follows that in some of our perceptions we directly experience not a material thing but a sense-datum. But sense-datum philosophers hold that not in some but all of our perceptions we are experiencing 'sense-data', because there is no distinction between those of our perceptions which are delusive, that is, in which we are under an illusion, and those which are veridical, that is, in which we are not under an illusion. For example, when I look at a straight stick, which is refracted in water and so appears bent, my experience of seeing it as bent is qualitatively similar to my experience of seeing a straight stick. And, my experience of seeing the white paper before me as red in red light is similar to my experience of seeing a red paper. There is no intrinsic property of perception on the basis of which we can make a distinction between veridical and delusive perceptions. Hence, in our normal perception too we directly experience nothing else but sense-data.

The argument from illusion can be reformulated as follows:

(i) Immediate sensory illusion does occur; that is, many a time it appears to us as if we were perceiving something, when nothing is present before us.

(ii) What we are aware of in an illusion is not objective, that is, not in the physical world.

(iii) Therefore, in illusion what we are directly aware of must be nothing but sense-data.

(iv) There is no qualitative difference between what we are aware of in our normal sense experience and what we are aware of when we experience an illusion.

(v) Hence, even in normal sense experience, we are directly aware of nothing but sense-data.

Let us now examine this argument. Though the premises (i) and (ii) express a truism, the premise (iii) does not follow from them. From the fact that in illusion what we are aware of is not in the public physical world, it does not follow that what we are aware of in illusion are sense-data.[16] The premise at (iv) is wrong. It is wrong because there is in fact a distinction between 'seeing' an illusory thing and seeing it in fact. This distinction is two-fold. Firstly, if there were no qualitative distinction between an illusion and a normal perception then every normal perception would be like an illusion. For example, if there were no qualitative distinction between a dream and a 'dreamlike quality', then the two could easily be used interchangeably. But this, in fact, is not so. Though it is true that illusions or dreams are narrated in the same terms in which ordinary perception or waking experiences are narrated yet it would be manifestly wrong to conclude from this that what is narrated, namely, the experience, in the two cases is exactly alike. It is a feature of our language that the same terms can often be used to describe different experiences. For example, when we are hit on the head, we say that we 'see stars'. But, this 'seeing stars' is qualitatively distinguishable from seeing stars when we look at the sky.[17]

Secondly, when we suffer from an illusion there is no object at all, physical or non-physical, which we are perceiving in any possible sense of 'perceiving'. We are simply under the false belief that ordinary perception is taking place. The difference between ordinary perception and sensory illusion is that in the case of ordinary perception the beliefs are true, whereas in the case of sensory illusions the beliefs are false. Moreover, in the case of illusion, we can if we wish say 'There is an object in my visual field' or 'I am having an after image — for instance, "seeing", a bright spot on the wall after I have removed my eyes from an electric arc'. These phrases do have their use. But we must remember that these expressions are 'systematically misleading' in philosophical contexts. They can, without loss of meaning, be easily replaced by statements like 'I falsely believe that I am perceiving something.'

One of the questions that can now be asked is, 'If sensory illusion were merely a matter of belief then why do we seem to ourselves to be perceiving something?' To answer this question, let us take the case of ordinary belief, namely, the belief that Figure 1.1 represents a smiling face, or the belief that there is a picture of an old woman spinning a *charkha* on the 'face' of the moon or the belief that the line (1) in the Müller-Lyer example (Figure 1.2) of an optical illusion is longer than the other line (2).

Figure 1.1

Figure 1.2

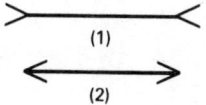

Now if I sincerely believe that Figure 1.3 represents a smiling face then it must seem to me that it is smiling, or that if I sincerely believe that there is a picture of an old woman spinning a *charkha*

Figure 1.3

on the face of the moon then it must seem to me to be so; or that if I sincerely believe that the line (1) in the Müller-Lyer example is longer than (2) then it must seem to me to be so. If it does not seem to me to be so then I would not believe it. All of us do recognise that in illusion our belief is false. Therefore, we do not say that there is a physical object or a state of affairs corresponding to it. But we trust our senses so deeply that we are not ready to admit that our belief is wholly false. So we postulate a 'sense-datum' and say that we do see something or have 'sense-data'. Thus, even if we grant that in illusion we are aware of sense-data, the conclusion at (v) namely, that in all our normal perceptions we are aware of sense-data, does not follow.

The argument from hallucination can be reformulated and demolished on the same lines as the argument from illusion. This, however, does not mean that hallucination and illusion stand for the same sort of experience. There is a distinction between a sensory illusion and a hallucination. In illusion, what we are aware of — say, the stick in the 'stick looks bent in water' example — does exist. In illusion error is involved only in the property that we assign to the object, or the particular property that we claim to be perceiving. But in the case of a hallucination, the object or the particular quality that we take to exist does not exist at all. For example, in the hallucinatory seeing of the cat on the mat, there is no cat on the mat at all, and in the hallucinatory seeing of a snake in the rope, there is no snake at all.

In the argument from illusion, or hallucination, sense-data were posited to explain hallucinations and sensory illusions, but in the next argument, the role of these theoretical entities is not merely to explain sensory illusion or hallucination but also to provide solid foundations for all our empirical knowledge. The philosophers who offer this argument assign sense-data the role of being the direct objects of awareness in our perception. They hold that our 'knowledge' of whatever we are directly aware of is incorrigible. Let us state and examine this argument, now.

The Argument from Verification or from Differential Certainty

The argument stated precisely proceeds along the following lines. (We shall construct the argument here, by taking the example of seeing only. The argument can similarly be constructed for hearing, smelling, tasting and other senses.) Whenever we see anything, say a tomato, we can always doubt whether what we are seeing is a tomato or a cleverly painted picture of tomato (Picasso once made the picture of the furniture on the interior walls of his house in such a way that to an onlooker it seemed to be a real piece of furniture), or only a wax piece, or whether we are not having a hallucination so that there is no object at all, in this case, a tomato. But, there is at least one thing that we cannot doubt, that there is a red, bulgy, circular or elliptical shape standing out from other colour patches or shapes — in short, there are sense-data of which we are directly aware. By saying that we are directly aware of them, as we have stated earlier,[18] we mean that sense-data are not reached via inference, or intellectual process. The argument from verification was clearly stated by H.H. Price. He says:

> When I see a tomato there is much that I can doubt. I can doubt whether it is a tomato that I am seeing, and not a cleverly painted piece of wax. I can doubt whether there is any material thing there at all. Perhaps what I took for a tomato was really a reflection; perhaps I am even the victim of some hallucination. One thing, however, I cannot doubt: that there exists a red patch of a round and somewhat bulgy shape, standing out from a background of other colour patches, and having a certain visual depth, and that this whole field of colour is directly present to my consciousness. What the red patch is, whether a substance, or a state of substance, or an event, whether it is physical or psychical or neither, are questions that we may doubt about. But that something is red and round then and there I cannot doubt. Whether the something persists even for a moment before and after it is present to my consciousness, whether other minds can be conscious of it as well as I may be doubted. But that it now *exists*, and that I am conscious of it — by me at least who am conscious of it this cannot possibly be doubted.[19]

The argument can be reconstructed as follows:

In my perception of tomato
   (i) It is not certain whether I am seeing a real tomato.
   (ii) It is certain that I am seeing something red and tomato shaped.

(iii) Since, what I am directly seeing or sensing, namely, the red, tomato-shaped something, cannot be identical with a tomato, therefore it must be sense-data.

(iv) We can construct the same argument with other sense perceptions also. Therefore, in all sense perception we are directly aware of nothing but sense-data.

We shall now examine the argument. It is quite obvious that the soundness of the argument depends upon the truth of (i) and (ii). The most important principle lying behind the two premises can be stated as follows: All empirical statements can be classified into two forms, namely, those that are certain and those that are not certain, simply by understanding what sort of claim they make about the way things are. The statements that fall under the former category are further sub-divided into those that are *intrinsically certain* or incorrigible, and those that are *not intrinsically certain*, or are corrigible. The example of those statements which are not intrinsically certain are statements of scientific hypothesis, generalisations, and even simple categorical statements like 'There is a tomato on the table' or 'The tomato is red' or 'The tomato is heavy.' There is no universal agreement on what sort of statements are to be called 'intrinsically certain'. Some philosophers, for instance, H.H. Price,[20] include statements that are about the 'observable properties' of things which are in the speaker's visual field, for example, the statement that there is something red and circular. Others would include only those statements that conform to the stringent formulae like 'It seems to me now exactly as though I were seeing something such and such' or 'that I apparently see something that looks such and such'.

But this principle is wrong. Firstly, because the truth and falsehood of an empirical statement, or a bunch of empirical statements, cannot be determined merely by looking at their formulation, or the things or episodes that they are supposed to describe. On the other hand, their truth and falsehood are determined relative to the context in which they are uttered. Secondly, there is not, in fact there cannot be, a single isolated statement which is incorrigible universally, that is, once uttered cannot be retracted or amended. It is held by sense-datum philosophers that statements couched in sentences such as 'It seems to me personally, here and now exactly as though I were seeing something red', are quite liable to amendment or retraction. The reason for calling the former statement incorrigible is that nothing whatever could actually be produced as cogent ground for retracting or amending it. But then, this is true not only of this form of statement but would be true of all those statements uttered by me in situations in which I am logically in the best possible position for making them. The kind of sentence that I make use of in making my statement has nothing to do with incorrigibility. What makes a statement incorrigible is the context in which I make it. So, there is no special class of statement which is as such incorrigible.

So far, we have shown that the general principle underlying premises (i) and (ii) is wrong. It follows, therefore, that (i) and (ii) also must be wrong. However, even if they were not wrong, it would not follow that they are absolutely incorrigible. This in turn means that the argument cannot establish the presence of a special kind of entities, namely, sense-data, the 'knowledge' of which is incorrigible. Thus, we are able to show that the first two premises of the argument are not sound. We propose now to show that the argument is logically invalid. It is invalid, for even if we grant the premises (i) and (ii) of the argument, the statement at (iii) does not follow from them. From the fact that what I am directly aware of is certainly red, round and tomato shaped, it does not follow that the red, tomatoish shaped thing is not identical with a tomato. Consider the following example:

> At dusk, when I see a blurred human figure at a distance from me, I am not absolutely certain whether the human figure out there is of my friend X or not. But from the fact that I am not absolutely certain about his being my friend X, does by no means follow that the human figure is not of my friend X.

Besides being invalid and having false premises, the argument is untenable on the grounds that it wrongly supposes that we infer the existence of material objects from sense-data. A typical formulation of this supposition is:

[(I am absolutely certain that I am sensing a red and tomato shaped sense-datum) ⊃ (I am seeing a tomato)]

But this is wrong, for we cannot infer the existence of material objects from the observation of sense-data. Such a theory implies that we can somehow jump from sense-data to the physical object itself. But only someone who was wearing inverting spectacles could accomplish such a feat. For, as we all know, we can only analyse perceptions in terms of theoretical entities — e.g. 'sense-data' — after we have already perceived those objects. That is, the theoretical analysis of the perception of physical objects in terms of 'sense-data' is dependent on the prior perception of those objects.

Let us now consider the next argument, namely,

The Argument from Causation, or Physiology of Perception

This proof for the existence of sense-data owes its allegiance to causal theory of perception, which in turn derives from scientific theories — from physics, especially optics and acoustics, which tell us about the propagation of light and sound waves; physiology, which tells us about the structure of the eye and the ear; and neurophysiology, which tells us about the transmission of impulses along the nerve fibres. A synthesis of these three scientific theories answers all our questions regarding the possibility, impossibility, efficiency, inefficiency of seeing and hearing. The philosophical argument can be divided into two parts:

(a) The argument from short causal chain.
(b) The argument from time lag.

(a) derives from physiology of perception, while (b) derives from the fact that light and sound waves have a finite velocity. We shall now consider these arguments one by one.

The Argument from Short Causal Chain

Stated precisely, it says: Science now gives us an account of how we see. It shows that before we perceive, a chain of processes has already taken place. The first link in the chain is the emission or reflection of light particles called photons from the object. These photons enter into the eyes of the perceiver and stimulate the retinal cells. These cells respond to the external stimulus and pass their signals via the optic nerve to the rear of the brain. Here in the 'visual area' of the brain, the signal is 'interpreted' and the 'image' formed. The perceiver does not see anything till these impulses have reached the brain (how this last step gives rise to seeing is not yet known). This stimulation of certain parts of the brain are then the last link of the chain that causes a person to perceive. Until this complex process has taken place no perception can occur. From this, it is inferred by philosophers that there can be no immediate perception of the physical objects or happenings around us. The only possible immediate objects of perception can be the last link in the causal chain of perception. Since this awareness is of nothing but the stimulation of certain brain cells which are far removed from the objects, precisely they are at the other end of causal chain, so that this awareness can only be of some representations, or images of objects. These representations, or images are nothing but sense-data. It is clear that in this argument sense-data are thought of as things impressed upon us, impulses transmitted through us, and not as things found by us by some deductive method. We shall now examine this argument.

Firstly, this whole argument rests on a logical howler in that it assimilates 'perception' to certain 'neural impulses' in the body. But, perception and neural impulses are quite different concepts. Perception, as we have said earlier,[21] is an acquired skill or is the exercise of an acquired skill, while a neural impulse is just a happening. It can be and possibly is a fact that certain neural impulses are necessary and sufficient pre-conditions for the occurrence of perception. But, the two are conceptually distinct and cannot be identified with each other, however closely they may be related. The hitting of light waves on my eyes and the resultant action in the brain cells make me see. But seeing is not identical with the hitting of light rays on my eyes, just as a beating stick makes me jump but my jumping is not identical with the beating stick. This observation is supported by the fact that we knew what perceiving was much before we knew about this complex process.

Secondly, this argument rests upon the mistaken idea that all our questions about perception are causal questions, that they are questions about the optics, physiology, and/or neurophysiology of seeing. Accordingly, it tries to 'explain' seeing and hearing in the way in which an earthquake is explained by a seismological theory, or diabetes is explained by a theory of pathology. But, all our questions about perceiving, particularly those which have an epistemological interest, are not causal questions, though some of them (for example, 'How do we see?') are and they are answered by relevant scientific theories. Those questions which are answered scientifically can be classified as technical questions. That we may ask technical questions besides causal questions in the context of an exercise of a skill can be illustrated by considerng the example of a wall-of-death performer. We can ask two different types of question in his case. The first are causal questions, for example, the mechanical questions about the speed, centrifugal and centripetal forces, physiological questions about the muscles, nerves and blood pressure of the performer, and the pedagogic questions about the training received and so on. The other type of question that we can ask may be questions about the nature of the performance, about the various types of mistake that are to be avoided and various types of attentives, and courage which make for success of the trick. These are the things which the performer must either have been taught by his trainers or have come to know by himself. The answer to this type of question cannot be given either by physicists, or chemists, or pathologists. Moreover, it is not necessary for a wall-of-death performer to know the answer to causal questions to perform the feat. Similarly, in the case of perceiving, which is the exercise of an acquired skill, questions about the crafts and arts of finding things out by seeing and hearing, questions about the nature of mistakes and failures in perception and their relations with mistakes and failures in thinking, spelling, counting and the like are those which we can ask besides causal questions.[22] These questions of technique cannot be answered by any multiplication of answers to questions of causal conditions. These two types of question are of quite different types. They belong to different categories.

In this argument from short causal chain, sense-data were postulated to supply the missing link in the causal chain of perception, to explain hearing, mishearing and non-hearing, little realising that question about the difference between them is a question about technique and not a causal question. No discovery or postulation of sense-data can give us what we want. Postulation of sense-data was aimed at solving a problem which really is not a causal problem. Nothing could be more wrong headed than this.

The Argument from Time Lag

This argument proceeds along the following lines: Physicists have discovered that light, sound, and electrochemical waves travel at a finite speed, such that the light emitted by the sun takes about eight minutes to reach us and in the case of some stars it takes years for it to reach us. From the causal chain of perception it follows that some time must lapse before we can perceive an object. In the case of some stars it can be years, in the case of hearing thunder it may be a few minutes, in the case of perceiving some distant light it may be a few seconds — in short, there is always a time gap, however small, before any particular state of affairs is perceived. This time lag can be infinitesimally small as in the case of objects at hand, but it cannot be zero. It is, therefore, logically possible that in the time taken by the light rays emitted by an object to stimulate certain brain cells, the object may instantaneously lapse into non-existence. But the perceiver would have the same visual presentation whether this miracle happens or not. It cannot be that he is directly aware of the object in either case. But how can we be directly aware now of what happened then? The past is over and gone. How can one see what is over and gone? To account for this time lag, philosophers thought that one must be aware of the image of the object, that is, one must be aware of the sense-data of the object. We shall now examine this argument.

At the outset, it must be noticed that the argument from time lag is virtually the same as the argument from short causal chain. The only difference between the two is that the latter involves space while the former involves time. The chain which originates in the emission of light rays by the object and ends in the stimulation of the brain cells creates not only a spatial gap between the first link and the last link but also a time lag between the two.

This argument trades on the common-sense belief that the events and the states of objects that we see must be simultaneous with our act of seeing them. The common-sense belief formulates this concept of immediate perception, because in paradigm cases of immediate perception, the objects perceived are at no great spatial distance, the events occur at the same time as the perception of them. From these cases we tend to make it a logical necessity that what I now immediately perceive must exist now. There is a contingent fact involved, a fact about the speed of reaction of our sensory apparatus relative to the physical events in our surroundings. Now, if the light travelled at much less speed than at what it travels now, our common sense would never have made such an erroneous assumption about simultaneous existence. The fact that we see the stars as they were many years ago comes as a shock to our common sense. But this does not force us to revise our conceptual system, because even with this new knowledge when we look at the stars, it still seems to us as if we were seeing a present event. All we need asserting is that what I immediately perceive now must seem to exist now. It is a fact that in movies we are directly presented with a continuous series of still pictures projected at a speed of 16 pictures a second, but this fact does in no way change the common-sense belief that what we see is moving pictures. Despite our knowledge of the fact that in a movie what we actually see are stationary pictures, we do not commonly say that we see stationary and not moving pictures. Therefore, this argument fails to demonstrate the truth of sense-datum theory.

These are all the major arguments offered by the defenders of the sense-datum theory to prove that we are directly confronted with sense-data in sense perception. We have been able to show that all these proofs are invalid.

We may now conclude our discussion on this topic with the following words of Ryle:

> in the ordinary contexts in which we talk about seeing, hearing and the rest, no mention is made of sense impressions, any more than in ordinary contexts in which meat, vegetables, and fruits are discussed, any mention is made of calories or vitamins. As I might put it the concept of perception is on a more elementary or less technical level than that of *sense-impression*. We can know all that is a part of common knowledge about seeing and hearing, without knowing anything about these impressions. But from this it follows directly that the concept of sense-impression is not any sort of component of the concept of perception, any more than the concept of *vitamin* is any sort of component of the concept of dinner.[23]

So far, we have been able to show negatively that sensations, sense-data or sense impressions are not the immediate objects of perception or in general of observation. The nearest we came to answer this question was when we said that observation entails having at least one sensation and paying heed to it. The next question that can now be asked is 'How does one pay heed?' But this question is analogous to the question 'How does one count?' or 'How does one walk?' As the latter questions are spurious questions so the former too must be spurious. And to a spurious question no answer can be given. So, we should not ask 'How does one pay heed?' rather we should ask 'What descriptions of an observer would count as his paying heed?' In answering this question we need not have any hypothesis or things which a person may have undergone privately. Even if he had undergone three or thirteen such processes, news about them would not explain what heeding or paying attention is. All we are interested to know is how the logical behaviour of one who pays heed differs from one who does not pay heed. We shall say a person has paid heed if he can recognise the things to which he paid heed at a subsequent time. Observing something entails not only seeing, hearing, touching, or smelling it but also paying heed.

Notes

1. Cf. G. Ryle, *The Concept of Mind*, Harmondsworth: Penguin Books, 1968 (henceforth referred to as 'CM'), p. 192.
2. CM, p. 192.
3. CM, p. 193.
4. CM, p. 204.
5. CM, p. 225.
6. Cf. D.M. Armstrong, *Perception and the Physical World*, London: Routledge & Kegan Paul, 1961, p. 5.
7. G. Ryle, 'Sensations', *Contemporary British Philosophy*, Third Series, ed. H.D. Lewis, London: George Allen & Unwin, 1956.
8. What I am considering here may be called 'the general theory of sense-data'.
9. *A Treatise on Human Nature*, Selby-Bigge Edition, 1967, Book I, Part I, Sec. 1, p. 1.
10. Cf. G. Ryle, 'Sensations'.
11. A.J. Ayer, *The Foundations of Empirical Knowledge*, London: Macmillan, 1953.
12. H.H. Price, *Perception*, London: Methuen, 1932.
13. B. Russell, *Our Knowledge of the External World*, London: Allen and Unwin, 1952.
14. *Perception*.
15. *The Foundations of Empirical Knowledge*.
16. We shall discuss this difficulty a little later in this chapter (see below, pp 26-27).
17. Cf. J.L. Austin, *Sense and Sensibilia*, Oxford: Clarendon Press, 1962.
18. See above, p. 16.
19. *Perception*, p. 3.
20. Ibid.
21. See above, pp. 11-13.
22. Cf. G. Ryle, 'Sensations'.
23. 'Sensations'.

2 PRIVACY AND PRIVATE LANGUAGE

We established in the previous chapter that we need not posit any private entities like sensations, sense impressions or sense-data to account for our observation. I try to show in this chapter that the individual needs no private, or any special language to register his thoughts, feelings and sensations. For we can, and in fact we always do register our sensations in the ordinary language. In arriving at this conclusion I have examined and exposed the errors, namely (a) the error about the nature of experience, and (b) the error about the nature of language, which underlie the mistaken view that we need a private language to register our thoughts, feelings, and sensations. In the end, I have maintained the thesis that the concept of a 'private language' rests on a category mistake.

Generally, a distinction is made between different notions of a private language.

There is the notion of a language which is private in the sense that it is understood by one person or a group of persons, for example, a code which is adopted by one person to write his views for his private use or a code which a group of people employ for the exclusive use of that group, as in the army. But this sort of code is not to be identified with private language, rather it is a private method of transcribing some given language.

A private language of this sort presents no philosophical problems, for it is derived from public language; and even if it were not, it will still be translatable into some public language. Its being private is just a matter of enough people knowing how to translate it. A 'private language' of this sort is not what philosophers talk about when they talk about private language.

There is the notion of a private language such that no one other than the speaker could understand it even if all the experiences of the speaker were available to others. This would be a language some features or other of which, irrespective of what the language is about, would make it logically impossible that any one other than the speaker should understand it or follow its rules. Though it is indeed hard to see how a language could possibly be such as to determine logically who should be capable of understanding it, and do that irrespective of what a person's experiences were.[1] This too is not the notion about which philosophers talk when they speak about private language.

There is the notion of a private language which cannot be taught to or learned by anyone other than the speaker, because it is a language which a particular person employs to refer only to his own private experiences. It is often held that a language is public if it refers to what is publicly observable; if a person could limit himself to describing his own sensations or feelings, then strictly speaking he alone would be able to understand what he was saying. This is the notion which philosophers in general, and Wittgenstein in particular, have in mind when they talk about private language. That Wittgenstein speaks about this notion of private language in the *Philosophical Investigations*[2] can be seen from the following two passages: 'The individual words of this language are to refer to what can only be known to the person speaking; to his immediate private sensations. So another person cannot understand the language' (*PI* 243); 'the language which describes my inner experiences and which only I myself can understand' (*PI* 256). The 'cannot' used in *PI* 243 is a logical 'cannot'. A private language is not the language of an imaginary soliloquist (solitary or in groups) but one whose concepts, rules, and opinions are essentially unsharable rather than contingently unshared. The essential characteristics of a private language thus are:

(a) The words of the language are to refer to what can only be known to the speaker.

(b) The words of the language are to refer to the speaker's immediate private sensations.

(c) Another person cannot understand the language.

We are now in a position to give a first approximation of our definition of 'private language':

Private language is a language that refers to the experiences of which only the speaker is aware and of which it is not merely the case that it is not understood by anyone other than the speaker, but more, that it is logically impossible that it should be understood by anyone other than the speaker. In *PI* 243 and 256 from which this definition is derived, it is not explicitly mentioned that the private language cannot have a single word in common with public language. But, Wittgenstein suggests this in *PI* 261:

What reason have we for calling 'S' the sign for a sensation? For 'sensation' is a word of our common language, not of one intelligible to me alone. And it would not help either to say that it need not be a *sensation*: that when he writes 'S' he has something — and that is all that can be said. 'Has' and 'something' also belong to our common language.

In fact, we may think of a private language having the same alphabets as ours. But having the words of our language is *ex hypothesi* ruled out. For, a word is not merely a collection of letters, but a collection whose use in the language is governed by syntactical and semantic rules of the language. A word can be compared with an atom, see Figure 2.1. An atom consists of a central part called a nucleus around which electrons revolve in a number of orbits. Similarly, a word consists of a sign or a sound or a collection of letters around which the rules revolve. These rules are part of the language game to which words belong. In order to understand the language one necessarily has to learn them. For example, it is necessary for one who wishes to learn Hindi that he learn the rules which govern the use of Hindi words. Just as electrons are integral parts of the atom, so are rules integral parts of the word (or language). And since a private language, logically, cannot be understood by anyone other than the speaker, its 'words' or 'expressions' cannot have public rules.[3] But words of our language have public rules. Therefore, private language cannot have any word in common with our public language.

Figure 2.1

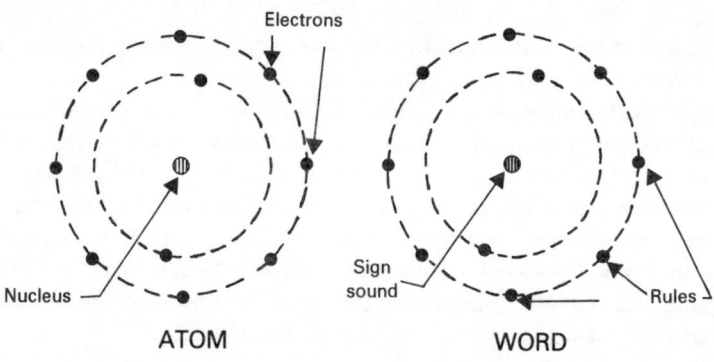

We have, now, one more characteristic of a private language, namely, that *it cannot have a single word in common with the public language*. To include this characteristic explicitly, we restate our definition of 'private language' as follows:
A private language is a language:

(a) which refers to the experience to which only its speaker has a privileged access;
(b) of which it is not merely the case that it is not understood by any one other than the speaker, but more, that it is logically impossible that it should be understood by anyone other than the speaker; and
(c) which cannot have a single word in common with the public language.

From this it follows that only one person, that is, the speaker of the language alone can be said to know the 'rules' of a private language. This is so because knowing a language entails knowing the rules of the language.

Carnap in his study *The Unity of Science*[4] gives the name 'Protocol language' to any set of sentences which are used to give a 'direct record' of one's own experiences. He argues:

> In general every statement in any person's protocol language would have sense for that person alone ... Even when the same words and sentences occur in various protocol languages, their sense would be different, they could not even be compared. Every protocol language could therefore be applied solipsistically: there would be no intersubjective protocol language. This is the consequence obtained by consistent adherence to the usual view and terminology (rejected by the author).[5]

Since Carnap wishes to maintain that protocol sentences should be understood by people, as this is the necessary condition for what he calls a 'physical language', he draws the conclusion that 'protocol language is a part of physical language'. That is, he concludes that sentences which *prima facie* refer to private experiences must be logically equivalent to sentences which describe the physical state of the subject. There are many other philosophers who have followed him in giving a physicalistic interpretation to the statements that one makes about the experiences of others. However, they have not extended it to all the statements that one may make about one's own experiences. They prefer to hold that certain sentences do serve only to describe the speaker's private experiences and that, this being so, they have a different meaning for him from any that they can possibly have for anyone else.

Wittgenstein goes much farther than this. He holds the view that one who attempts to use a private language not only fails to communicate his meaning to others, but also does not have a meaning to communicate even to himself; in other words, he does not succeed in saying anything at all.

Wittgenstein considered that the notion of a private language rested on two fundamental mistakes. They are: (i) mistake about the nature of experience; and (ii) mistake about the nature of language. The mistake about the nature of experience is the belief that experiences are private; that is, no one can know that another person is in pain or is dizzy, or has any other sensation. For, sensations are thought to be private in the sense that no one can experience or be acquainted with another person's sensations.[6]

This mistake leads to the mistake about language, namely, the belief that words acquire meaning by bare ostensive definition; that is, no one can be taught the names of sensations unless he has those sensations himself. On this view, each one of us must give the sensation words meaning from his own case independently of others and of other people's use of similar words. From this, it follows that anyone who says anything (or who uses any sound or sign) about his sensations says something which he alone can understand. Therefore, 'names' of sensations or sensation words, the word 'sensation' itself, and the expression 'same sensation' will have no public but only a private use.

According to Wittgenstein, the belief that experiences (sensations) are private rests on a confusion of two senses of 'privacy'. The first sense of 'privacy' has to do with *knowledge*. In this sense, something is private to me if and only if I alone can know about it (*vide PI* 246). The second sense of privacy has to do with *possession*. In this sense, something is private to me if and only if I can have it. The first sense of privacy may be abbreviated as *incommunicability* and the second sense as *inalienability*. The question 'Are sensations private?', then, breaks up into two sub-questions:

(i) 'Are sensations incommunicable?'
(ii) 'Are sensations inalienable?'

We shall now try to answer these questions one by one.

The line of argument of those who hold that sensations are incommunicable may be formulated as follows:

(i) Anyone who has a sensation knows that he has it because he feels it; and whatever can be known to exist by being felt cannot be known (in the same sense of 'know') to exist in any other way.

(ii) The proper and necessary means of coming to know what sensations another person is having is to feel (have) that person's sensations.

(iii) No one can feel (experience, or be acquainted with) another person's sensations. Therefore:

(iv) No one can know what sensations another person is having.

Let us call this argument (A). It is clear that premises at (i) and (ii) are the crux of the argument. We shall try to show that (i) and (ii) make a spurious use of the verb 'to know' and therefore, are false. Since the conclusion stated at (iv) also makes use of 'know' in the same sense, this too is false.

For clarity's sake, Wittgenstein considers a particular sensation, namely, pain, in the argument against the possibility of private language. He takes this example because pain is the commonest sensation and, in many ways, the most difficult of all the sensations to deal with. It is also one of the first such words to be learnt, and one which may well form a basis for the future extension of sensation vocabulary.[7]

The premises at (i) and (ii) can, then, be reconstructed as: (ir) Anyone who has pain knows that he has it because he feels it, and whatever can be known to exist by being felt cannot be known (in the same sense of 'know') to exist in any other way. (iir) The proper and necessary means of coming to know the pain another person is having is to feel (have) that person's pain. From these premises, it follows that I can know that I am in pain because I feel my pain, and that if anybody else wants to know about my being in pain, then the only way for him is to feel my pain. These expressions, thus, presuppose that there is a genuine use of the verb 'to know' as an expression of certainty in the first person psychological statements. This forms the foundation of the argument, since the conclusion (iv) says that no one can know in the sense of first person assertion of 'know' the sensations which the other person is having. If we are able to prove that this is a spurious use of the verb 'to know', then we should reject not only (i) and (ii) but also the conclusion of the argument.

Consider a case in which 'I know that' becomes an expression of certainty. It is the rainy season. You have come to my place to play chess with me. The game is about to finish. You, while still absorbed in the game, ask my younger brother who is sitting near the window, 'Is it raining?' He says, 'It is'. And then you ask, 'Are you certain?' He might reply, 'Yes, I know it is raining, I am looking out of the window.' Now, the function of the words 'I know' here is that in answering the question 'Is it raining?' one (in this case, my brother) is not merely guessing or taking someone's words for granted, or is not judging from what he saw ten minutes ago, but that he is in a position, as one would want, to answer this question. The addition of the words 'I know' here makes it an expression of certainty, for it is quite intelligible for someone else to suppose that the speaker is not in as good a position as is required for answering the question 'Is it raining?'

Let us now imagine another case. We have finished the game of chess. It is time for you to leave. You ask my younger brother, who is sitting near the window, 'Is it raining?' You look at him. He opens the window, puts his hand out, and as he closes the window, wiping the drops from his hand, says, 'Yes, it is raining.' Now, since you have seen him taking the necessary pains to answer your question, you would have nothing to gain by asking 'Are you certain?' or 'Do you really know that it is raining?' For the reason that he would not be telling you anything more by the addition of the words 'I know that ...' because the addition of the words 'I know' properly means "There is no such thing as a doubt in this case" or "The expression 'I do not know' makes no sense in this case." And of course it follows from this that "I know" makes no sense either'.[8]

Therefore, the addition of the words 'I know' is pointless and redundant. Hence for 'I know that ...' to be an expression of certainty, it should at least be conceivable in some circumstances that the sense of the sentence filling in the blanks allows the speaker to be ignorant of the truth-value of the statements made by the use of the sentence. The addition of the words 'I know' makes sense only when a doubt is possible. In cases in which no doubt is possible the use of the words 'I know' is pointless. Moreover, we can use 'I know' profitably only in the cases in which it makes sense to ask the question 'How do you know?' This question, generally, is asked in those cases in which the question of learning is involved. For example, in the case of 'It is raining', a person can, if he has not seen the speaker taking the necessary pains, before making the reply, ask, 'How do you know that it is raining?' or 'How do you learn that it is raining?'

In light of the above discussion, let us now try to see whether the use of 'I know' in the case of first person present tense psychological expressions, for example, 'I am in pain', can be an expression of certainty as is supposed by the premises (ir) and (iir) of the argument.

At the outset, it must be made clear that there are some non-philosophical contexts in which 'I know I am in pain' is not unintelligible. For instance, a man has been complaining for several days that he has a severe pain in his throat, but has not sought any relief from it. His wife has been constantly nagging him, 'You're in pain; so why not see a doctor?' He may sometimes say to her in exasperation, 'I know I am in pain, but we cannot afford a doctor.' No one would like to maintain that this expression of exasperation was unintelligible. What we want to show, however, is not that the words 'I know' in the first person psychological sentences can be used as an expression of exasperation, but that they cannot be used as an expression of certainty.

Now, for 'I know' to qualify as an expression of certainty, the following conditions should be satisfied:

(i) There could, in principle, be a doubt about the ignorance of the speaker about the truth-value of the statement expressed by the sentence attached with it, that is, there could be a doubt about the assertion.

(ii) The question 'How do you know?' could be asked about the contents of the sentence attached with 'I know'; and, an answer could be given to this question. For example, in the case of 'It is raining', one can ask 'How do you know?' The answer can be 'I know, because I see through the window that it is raining', 'I know because my hands became wet when I put them out of the window.'

However, in the case of first person psychological assertion, for example, 'I am in pain', there cannot, in principle, be a doubt that the speaker of these words is ignorant about the truth-value of the contents, viz:, his being in pain. He knows, when he says it, whether he has a pain or he is only saying it without having the pain. A doubt can arise in those cases only in which one is learning. For example, in the case of continuing the series 1, 3, 5, 7, 9 ..., one can doubt not only whether the person has learnt how to go on but also whether he himself shall be able to go on correctly.

But the case of sensations is different. In their case 'I cannot be said to learn of them. I have them' (*PI* 246). And I cannot doubt those things which I have. For example, I cannot doubt whether there is a pen in my pocket if I have it in my pocket. 'It makes sense to say about other people that they doubt whether I am in pain but not to say it about myself' (*PI* 246). For other people this (doubt) makes sense, because they learn of my being in pain either from my behaviour and/or from my sincere utterances of the words 'I am in pain'. But in my own case it does not make sense, because I do not learn of them, I have them. As in the case of 'It is raining', it makes no sense for the person who sees from the window, or who is walking in the rain to doubt whether it is raining.

To further clarify our position let us look at the way we teach a child the usage of the word 'pain'. A child whenever he has pain cries; the adults who already know 'pain', after looking at the symptoms of pain, tell him to use the word 'pain', whenever he has pain which he expressed by crying previously. The word 'pain' replaces the primitive natural expression of pain, that is, a cry. Thus the sentence 'I am in pain' instead of being a description of a mental state, is more like a cry of complaint (*vide PI*, page 189, part ii). Since 'I am in pain' is like a cry of complaint, 'I doubt whether I am in pain' is senseless in the same way as 'I doubt whether to utter ouch!' or 'I doubt whether to utter Hurrah!' In the situation in which it is senseless to say 'I doubt whether ...' it always is equally senseless to say 'I know that ...'. This can be seen if we compare 'I am in pain' with an order, an exclamation, or a wish — e.g., 'Shut the door!', 'Good morning!', or 'Hurrah!' 'I doubt whether 'good morning' is as senseless as 'I know that good morning' and 'I doubt whether shut the door' is as senseless as 'I know that shut the door', and 'I doubt whether Hurrah' is as senseless as 'I know that Hurrah.' Because in the case of 'good morning!' it is not just psychologically, but logically impossible to doubt whether good morning. Therefore it does not make sense to talk of knowledge and certainty of 'good morning'. Similarly in the

case of 'I am in pain', it is not just psychologically but logically impossible to doubt whether I am in pain. Therefore, it is senseless to talk of knowledge and certainty of 'I am in pain.'
Since it is out of place to talk of knowledge and certainty in the case of 'I am in pain', the question 'How do you know?' also becomes senseless. For, a question can sensibly be asked when there is a context of knowledge or learning. For example, in the case of continuing the series 1, 3, 5, 7, 9 ..., we can ask 'How do you know?' The answer can be 'By working on the formula a + (n−1)d.' But, in the case of 'I am in pain' the question 'How do you know?' cannot be asked. For it can be asked in those cases only in which a doubt exists; and in which 'an answer exists and an answer (can exist) only where something can be said' (*TLP* 6.51). We have already seen that there is no place for doubt in the case of 'I am in pain.' And what sort of answer can we imagine to the question 'How do you know that you are in pain?' The difficulty in answering this question is analogous to the following example:

> If a blind man were to ask me 'Have you got two hands?', I should not make sure by looking. If I were to have any doubt of it, then I do not know why I should trust my eyes. For, why should not I test my *eyes* by looking to find out whether I see my two hands? *What* is to be tested for *what*? (Who decides *what* stands fast). And what does it mean to say that such and such stands fast (*OC* 125).

In fact, in 'I am in pain' there simply is not the question 'How?' as in 'Why do I not satisfy myself that I have two feet when I want to get up from a chair? There is no why. I simply do not. This is how I act' (*OC* 148).

However, one of the answers that may be suggested to the question 'How do you know that you are in pain?' is 'I know that I am in pain by feeling it.' Let us now consider this answer. We shall concentrate on the grammar of the verb 'feel'.

There is a perceptual sense of the verb 'to feel' as in 'I feel a stone in my shoe.' But, when we use the verb 'feel' in the first person psychological assertions (e.g., in 'I feel a slight pain in my knee when I bend it'), it is not used in the perceptual sense; for the words 'I feel' can easily be substituted by the words 'there is' or 'I have'. Such a substitution is not possible in the case of 'I feel a stone in my shoe' by 'There is a stone in my shoe.' While the former implies the latter, it does not mean the same. Whereas the assertion 'There was a stone in my shoe but I did not feel it' makes sense, the assertion 'There was a pain in my knee but I did not feel it' makes no sense. Further, if we try to answer 'How do you know that you are in pain?' by 'Because I feel it!' then we enter into a vicious circle, and give no explanation at all. As Wittgenstein put it:

> 'How do you know that you have pain?' Because 'I feel them'. But I feel them means the same as 'I have them'. Therefore this was no explanation at all.[9]

In fact, our knowing that we are in pain is sufficient criterion for our knowing that we are in pain. As can be seen from the following parallel example:

> 'How do you know that you have raised your arm?' — 'I feel it'. So what you recognise is the feeling? And are you certain that you recognise it right? — You are certain that you have raised your arm; isn't this the criterion, the measure, of recognition (*PI* 625).

The reason for entering into this vicious circle is that when we ask 'how?' we make a mistake of looking 'for an explanation where we ought to look at what happens as a "proto-phenomenon". That is, when we ought to have said: *this language game is played*' (*PI* 654).

We have been able to show that the sensation words cannot be the objects of the verbs of perception in first person psychological statements. Therefore, the arguments given by those who hold that sensations are private in the sense that nobody other than the one who feels them becomes quite implausible.

In our discussion so far, we have shown that the alleged use of the expression 'I know' as an expression of certainty is a spurious use. It follows then that the premises (i) and (ii) of the argument (A) are false. Since the conclusion at (iv) also makes use of the same sense of 'know' that (i) and (ii) do, it also is false. In the ordinary sense of 'know', people know when I am in pain and also I know when other people are in pain. This can easily be seen from our day-to-day experiences when we pass judgements on the 'inner states' of others and are right. Judgements of this kind depend upon the good evidence available to us.

One of the reasons for the sceptic to say that we can never pass correct judgements about the 'inner states' of others is the possibility of pretence or shamming by other persons. To this, Wittgenstein would reply that some types of behaviour cannot be said to fall under the concept of pretending, or shamming. One's ground for judgement of such acts can be empirical. For example, there can be no doubt of pretence about the pain of a man who after being crushed under a car is lying in a pool of blood and is crying 'I am in pain'.

Pretence, or shamming, which characterises the pretended action, for example, pain behaviour, is an acquired skill. Only those who are already familiar with the forms of behaviour, can pretend to have pain when in fact they do not have it. Since infants and animals lack the mastery of those skills, the supposition of pretence is senseless in their case; and 'to suppose that all behaviour might always be pretence is to suppose that the concept of pretending might lack behavioural criteria and that is not possible.[10] Or as Ryle puts it: 'the menace of shamming is an empty menace. We know what shamming is. It is deliberately behaving in ways in which other people behave who are not shamming' (*CM*, p. 166).

Now, the sceptic may ask, 'Granted that I can know the "inner states" of others, can I know them with the same certainty as applies to other things?' To this Wittgenstein replies: 'I can be as *certain* of someone else's sensations as of any fact.' (*PI* II, p. 224) But this certainty is of a completely different kind from that which is expressed in a proposition such as '25 × 25 = 625'. The difference here, however, is logical, not psychological. To be sure, our feelings of certainty — of the absence of doubt — may well be the same. The criterion for our feeling certain about a matter lies in our behaviour, and so far as that is concerned we are no less certain in general about the 'inner states' of others than about the mathematical judgements of the sort 'Twice two is four.'

The sceptic confuses the logical kinds of certainty (for instance, the deductive proof of the justification of a mathematical theorem) with the different kinds or degrees of psychological certainty. He forgets that mathematical certainty is not a psychological concept. And that the kind of certainty that is required in different language games depends upon the kind of language game involved, e.g., the kind of certainty required in continuing the series 1, 2, 3 ... up to 10 is my success in continuing it (cf. *PI*, part II, p. 224) and the kind of certainty required in my remembering a person is my success in recognising the person when I meet him next. He assumes that there is one and only one concept, or meaning or kind of certainty. But this assumption is mistaken for we have various concepts or meanings or kinds of certainty. The kind of certainty required in mathematics is different from the kind of certainty required in psychology; the kind of certainty required in history is different from the kind of certainty required in sociology. Correspondingly the criterion or criteria of certainty also varies from one context to the other. What counts as a criterion of certainty therefore, is not fixed but is variable — it varies according to the requirements of the situation.

To sum up: we have so far shown that sensations are not incommunicable — that is, we can know when others are in pain or what sensations, if any, they are having, and also that others can know what sensations, if any, I am having.

Let us now turn to the inalienability sense of 'privacy' according to which my sensations are private to me in the sense that only I can have them. This sense is expressed in the premise (iii) of argument (A) where it is said 'No one can feel (experience, or be acquainted with) another person's sensation.' Here Wittgenstein asks two questions:

(i) Which are my pains?
(ii) What counts as criterion of identity here? (*PI* 253).

The first question is a request for the criterion of possessing pain, whereas the second question asks for the criterion of identity of pain.

The question (i) is like the question about a material object, e.g., 'Which is my room?', 'Which is my table?', 'Which is my coat?' The answers can be 'The room near the staircase on the third floor is your room', 'The table near the window in that room is your table', and 'The second coat in the wardrobe is your coat.' In such questions, therefore, the spatial location of the material object provides, in general, a principle of individuation for the object in question. Thus, in reply to the question (i), one is apt to answer, 'My pains are the pains felt in my body', or 'Any pains which I feel are my pains.' This is the answer against which

Wittgenstein constantly argues. According to him, it rests on two mistakes:

(i) It supposes that this is a truth about the nature of pains or of human beings, that only one in whose body it is located can feel it.

(ii) It supposes that the word 'mine' is a possessive of ownership as 'my' in 'He has my coat.'

Against the first mistake Wittgenstein argued repeatedly and held that one could quite conceivably feel pain in someone else's body (*BB* p. 68). In order to show that the first premise is mistaken, and that one could in principle feel pain in someone else's body, Wittgenstein demonstrates that there is no *logical contradiction* in such a supposition. Indeed, there are many cases in actual life where such expressions are perfectly intelligible. For example, when I see a man crushed under a car and bleeding profusely, I say 'Oh! It is painful.' I say the same thing when a man with an injured left hand comes to me. But, when I am asked to touch the spot of pain, I touch the injured part of the person who has been hit by the car or the left hand of the person in the latter case. This would naturally be the pain felt in another's body. So, my pain is not necessarily the pain felt in my body. The criterion of ownership of pain, therefore, is not given by the location of the pain in the body, but by the pain behaviour of the person who gives it expression. *He who manifests pain is its owner.* And, the pain which I manifest may single out a place outside my body.

Let us now consider the second mistake. 'My pain', 'his pain', 'your pain' look like expression of ownership because of the surface similarity with 'my coat', 'his coat', 'your coat'. But this analogy is false; because in order to use a possessive of ownership as in 'his coat', 'my coat', and the like, and to make a true statement, we must identify correctly the owner of the article. It is this identification which makes a difference between saying 'His coat is too large for him' and saying that 'That coat is too large for him.' If I had without identifying correctly said, 'His coat is too large for him', then I could be corrected by saying 'That is not his coat, it is his father's.' Here 'he' and 'his' are not performing the same function. 'He' shows the person, whereas 'his' shows the owner, the possessor.

In the case of sensations, in order to be in a position to use correctly the expression 'his sensations' it is sufficient to know who is in pain. There is no other step required comparable to that of the correct identification of the owner as in 'his coat'. In fact the question of identification does not have a place in the language game played with the sensation vocabulary:

> There is no question of recognising a person when I say I have a toothache. To ask 'Are you sure that it is *you* who have pain?' would be nonsensical. Now when in this case no error is possible, it is because the move which we might be inclined to think of as an error a 'bad move' is no move of the game at all. (We distinguish in chess between a good and bad moves, and we call it a mistake if we expose the queen to a bishop. But it is no mistake to promote a pawn to a king.) (*BB* 67).

In the case of sensations, the talk of correct identification of the possessor is senseless (non-sensical), not because a particular combination of words is ruled out in the language game, but because an attempt is being made to make a move with the help of this group of words in a language game whereas it in fact belonged to the other language game. As Wittgenstein is said to have remarked:

> Where we say 'this makes no sense', we always mean 'This makes nonsense *in this particular game*'; and in answer to the question 'why do we call it "nonsense"? What does it mean to call it so?' said that when we call a sentence 'nonsense', it is 'because of some similarity to sentences which have sense, and that 'nonsense always arises from forming symbols analogous to certain uses, where they have no use'.[11]

Moreover, in 'My pain is quite severe', the word 'My' is performing the same function as 'I' in 'I am in severe pain'. But as we have seen in the case of possessive of ownership, 'My' and 'I' are to perform different functions. Therefore, the word 'mine' in 'The pains that I have are mine' is not the possessive of ownership. Hence, 'The pains that I have are mine' can be replaced by 'my pains'. Thus the word 'my' in 'my pain' is not to be thought of as a possessive of ownership.

If the question 'Which are my pains?' prompts us to answer it by saying, 'Any pain that I have is mine', then both the question and the answer should be recognised as spurious, as not belonging to the language game. 'My pains' (not in the sense of possessive of ownership) are the pains which I express, or perhaps the pains which if expressed would necessarily be expressed by me (cf. *PI* 302).

The question 'What is the criterion of identity for pains?' implies 'How are the pains, such as toothache, headache and others, distinguished from each other?' The answer is: by their phenomenal characteristics such as their intensity and location. If these phenomenal characteristics are the same, then it is possible for both of us, or for that matter for all of us, to have the same pain. For example, if both of us feel a sharp pain in the upper abdomen an hour after taking the same food, then it is perfectly natural for both of us to say that we have the same pain.

It may be objected that this is not absolutely correct, since the pains are not felt literally in the same place but only in corresponding places in two different bodies. To this Wittgenstein would reply that it is possible for the Siamese twins to have the pain exactly in the same place, namely, the place where they are joined together. Besides, it is not in the least logically incorrect to say that two persons have pain in the same place. Here, it may again be objected by a sceptic that pains are not specifically the same in the sense that they are numerically different: for one is Tweedledee's pain and the other is Tweedledum's pain. But, we point out, this is making the possessor a characteristic of pain which, as we have shown above, is a mistake. Therefore, the criterion of counting pains as 'my pain', 'his pain', 'Tweedledee's pain', 'Tweedledum's pain' is wrong. When one counts pains one counts differently. The criterion of enumeration of pains is different from the criterion of counting objects. While the case of the latter one can take into account the possessor (owner) as an identifying mark — for example, 'my pen' and 'his pen' refer to two pens — in the case of the former the possessor or owner cannot be regarded as an identifying mark — for example, 'my toothache' and 'his toothache' are not two toothaches. In the case of pains one counts in a way in which one counts colours, habits, gaits and the like, we count in these cases with more or less detailed descriptions. This can be illustrated by the following example.

A five-gaited horse is one that can ambulate in five descriptions of foot movements; and two horses have the same gait if these foot movements fit the same relevant description. To say that they are performing two gaits which are exactly alike does not make sense.

What would count as two gaits is some difference in the foot movements of two horses. Similarly a person has the same pain, if he fits the same (relevant) description; and if a hundred people fit the same description, then all of them have the same pain.

The confusion about identity lies in the mistake of thinking that the same is same always, that the use of the word 'same' is governed by the same fixed rule irrespective of the context; whether we may be talking of 'coats', 'tables', 'pains', 'gaits', or 'sensations'. This is the mistake made by Ayer when he writes: 'physical objects are public because it makes sense to say of different people that they are perceiving the same physical object; mental images are private because it does not make sense to say of different people that they are having the same mental image, they can be imagining the same thing but it is impossible that their respective images should be literally the same.'[12]

The talk of 'literally' being the same makes the use of the word 'same' as if it had one and the same meaning in all contexts. The mistake lies in not seeing the 'same' must always be understood not in an abstract and pure sense but together with some general term such as pain, or coat, and that the criterion of identity in any particular case is determined by the general term involved. For example, when we talk of the identity of chairs (physical objects), we use 'same' and 'exactly alike' interchangeably, as in 'This chair is identical with that', 'This chair is exactly like that', or 'This chair is the same as that.' Here we are talking of two chairs. When we talk of the identity of physical objects we talk of two or more things. But, in the case of the identity of colours, when we say, 'This colour here is exactly 'like the colour over there', or 'This is the same colour here as over there', whichever of them we say, there is but one colour — say, red — and it would be a mistake to say 'There cannot be only one colour; for there is a colour here and also that colour there.'

The case of pains is not like phsyical objects but is like colours. To assimilate pains to physical objects is to make a 'category mistake'. It would be a mistake to think that when we talk of two people having the same pain, say pain in the upper abdomen, 'same pain' here means 'two pains being exactly alike'. As Wittgenstein says: 'In so far as it makes *sense* to say that my pain is the same as his, it is also possible for us both to have the same pain' (*PI* 253).

It follows, then, that it is possible for two people to have the same pain as for two surfaces to have the same colour. But, somebody defending the thesis that 'Sensations are inalienable' may strike himself on the breast and say, 'But surely another person cannot have this pain' (*PI* 253). Therefore, only I can have my pains.

The statement 'Only I can have my pains' is equivalent to 'If they are my pains, I have them.' But this is an analytic statement like 'One plays patience by oneself' (*PI* 248). Therefore, this statement is comparatively uninformative about pains. Moreover, 'Only I can have my pains' is not true particularly of pains but of many other things besides pains, e.g., blushes, sneezes, catches and the like. If you blush, then surely it is your blush, and if you sneeze, then surely it is your sneeze, it is not mine, nor anybody else's. If on the cricket field the catch comes to mid-on position, the position at which you are standing, then surely it is your catch and not mine or any other player's. If somebody wants to maintain that blushes and sneezes are inalienable in this sense, then this is a very tenuous sort of privacy, and so is the case with the one who maintains that sensations are inalienable. This, however, does not make sensations any more private than behaviour.

Someone may still object and say that there is one sense in which pains are more private than behaviour, namely, that they can be kept secret without being publicly manifested in any way. If one wants to call an experience thus kept to oneself private — for example, a chess move considered and discarded in imagination — then there clearly are such private experiences. Nobody, including Wittgenstein, denies this sort of privacy to experiences. From this, it follows that there are some experiences which are private because they are kept to oneself. But the fact that there are some such experiences does not entail that all experiences are private in this sense. If a man itches, but does not scratch or report his itch, we may call that a private experience. But, if he scratches or reports his itch, there is no reason for us to call his itch private. So in this sense of 'private' some of our pains are private and others are not. And from the mere fact that some pains are private in this sense it does not follow that all pains are private. 'What sometimes happens could always happen' is a fallacy (cf. *PI* 345). 'Some money is forged but it could not be that all money was forged.'[13] These considerations are, thus, sufficient to prove the thesis that sensations have no special inalienability.

We have shown above that our answer to the question 'Are

sensations incommunicable?' is 'No'; and also our answer to the question 'Are sensations inalienable?' is 'No; not in any sense peculiar to sensations.' These two questions were part of the question 'Are sensations private?' Since our answer to both is in the negative, the answer to the question 'Are sensations private?' is also in the negative. It follows that our experiences are not private. It is quite possible for people to know that another person is in pain or is dizzy or has any other sensation.

Let us now turn to the second mistake that the supporter of 'private language' makes, namely, that sensation-specifying terms acquire meaning, that they can be taught, and used by private ostensive definition. We can make a list of sensation-specifying terms, or the terms, or words, that mean kinds of sensations: 'itch', 'ache', 'pain', 'toothache', 'headache', 'stomach ache', 'muscular ache', 'smarting', 'throbbing pain', 'burning sensation', 'dizziness', 'tickle', 'tingling', 'bitter taste', 'nausea', 'fluish feeling', 'ringing in the ears', 'bright image'. One can add many more. All these are quite familiar and are of long standing. For the reasons already stated earlier, we shall take the example of 'pain'.

Wittgenstein's criticism of the mistake can be divided into two parts:

(i) The first part is concerned with the concept formation or acquisition of a concept.

(ii) The second part is concerned with the retention of a concept.

The first mistake that a private linguist makes is the claim that he can name his sensation by a private ostensive definition, that he can form a concept S of a sensation by means of associating a word 'S' with the occurrence of the sensation S. The word 'S' was hitherto indefinable, but he gives it a stipulative definition by mental ostentation. From this it follows that he treats the sensation S as the object, and the word 'S' as its name.[14]

Wittgenstein objects to this account on two grounds. First, naming, that is, forming a new concept bringing a particular object or the incarnation of some general characteristics under a general concept expressed by means of words presupposes a variety of complex conditions. As Wittgenstein says:

What does it mean to say that he has 'named his pain' — How has he done the naming of pain? And whatever he did, what was its purpose? — When one says 'He gave a name to his sensations' one forgets that a great deal of stage setting in the language is presupposed if the mere act of naming is to make sense. And when we speak of someone's having given a name to pain, what is presupposed is the existence of the grammar of the word 'pain', it shows the post where the new word is stationed (*PI* 257).

In the case of a private linguist there is *ex hypothesi* no such stage-setting, there is no grammar to show us the 'post' where the new word, say 'S', which names the sensation S is to be stationed. Therefore 'naming' in a private linguist theory makes no sense. (In the course of this discussion, I shall show also that even if naming in a private linguist's theory had made some sense, he would not have been able to consistently use it.)

Secondly, Wittgenstein denies that words such as 'pain', 'itch', 'tickle' and the like name private sensations. In *Zettel* Wittgenstein's wayward self says 'Joy' surely designates an inward thing, and his sterner self replies 'No! "Joy" designates nothing. Neither any inward nor any outward thing' (*Z* 487). We must, however, make it clear that he is not denying that there is a trivial sense in which 'pain' is the name of a sensation. In this sense 'pain' denotes a sensation as 'five' denotes a number, or as 'understanding' denotes a mental process, and as obviously every word denotes something or the other. For instance, 'pain' is a sensation word; and it has uses closely allied to the other sensation words, as for instance 'itch' and 'tickle', just as 'five' is a number word and has uses closely allied to other number words, as for example 'one', 'two', 'three', and 'four'.

The genesis of the idea that 'pain' is the name of a sensation is that we talk about pains very much as we talk about colours, sounds, and textures. For example, we refer to people and attribute sensations to them as in the locutions 'He is in pain', 'You are in pain', 'I am in pain' in the same way as we refer to objects and attribute colours to them in 'That is red', 'This book is red.' So, we come to think that the naming relation in the two must be very much the same.

The first absurd consequence of the idea that 'pain' is the name of a private sensation is that the proposition 'he is in pain' assumes that the person referred to has a particular sensation before his consciousness, which I cannot have or feel. Since I cannot have his sensation of pain, I can never know whether he has pain or not. We have shown earlier that it is quite possible for us to know with almost the same certainty with which we know '$2 \times 2 = 4$', that another person is in pain.

Next, if 'pain' is the name of a sensation which I only experience in the privacy of my consciousness, then the propositions 'He is in pain' or 'You are in pain' would be unintelligible to me. For, if 'pain' denotes an item of my consciousness, for me, then pain can exist only when I am aware of it. It makes no sense to say that I no longer feel the pain yet it is going on all the same. On this view, therefore, the essential characteristic of pain is that I feel it, and I would be guilty of contradicting myself if I said that there is pain which I do not feel, but which another person feels. One possible objection to this view may be that though it is true that I only know what pain is from my own case, surely I can imagine that someone else feels the same as I feel when I have pain, when he says 'I am in pain', or 'He is in pain.' Wittgenstein replies to this:

'But if I suppose that someone has a pain, then I am simply supposing that he has just the same as I have so often had'. — That gets us no further. It is as if I were to say: 'You surely know what "it is 5 o'clock here" means; so you also know what "It is 5 o'clock on the sun" means. It means simply that it is just the same time there as it is here when it is 5 o'clock.' — The explanation by means of *identity* does not work here. For I know well enough that one can call 5 o'clock here and 5 o'clock there 'the same time', but what I do not know is in what case one is to speak of its being the same time here and there.

In exactly the same way, it is no explanation to say that he has a pain is simply the supposition that he has the same as I. For *that part* of grammar is quite clear to me that is, that one will say that the stove has the same experience as I, *if* one says it is in pain and I am in pain (*PI* 350).

The reason for our inability to imagine what it would be like at 5 o'clock in the afternoon on the sun is that the very notion of being a certain time, of being 5 o'clock, or 7 o'clock, presupposes a system of time zones. And, one can speak of its being a particular time only for a particular time zone, as for example 5 o'clock in the afternoon in India, in America, or in France. But we cannot talk of its being 5 o'clock in the afternoon on the earth. In short, the concept '5 o'clock in the afternoon on the sun' does not have a stage-setting in the language game. We do not know where the concept is stationed. Similarly, if 'pain' is the name of a sensation, then I cannot conceive that another person feels the same sensation as I do when I feel pain, though I may imagine all sorts of images in connection with those words. Part of my imagining that another person experiences the same private sensation which I feel when I have pain is that I imagine him feeling a private sensation. But, how can I do this? we might say that he has the private sensation which I feel when I have pain, but,

> this is none too easy a thing to do: for I have to imagine pain which *I do not feel* on the model of the pain which *I do feel.* That is, what I have to do is not simply to make a transition in imagination from one place of pain to another. As, from pain in the hand to pain in the arm. For I am not to imagine that I feel pain in some region of his body (which would also be possible) (*PI* 302).

There are no specifiable conditions under which I could determine that another person feels the same sensation as I do. For to feel that, I have to feel his pain. But this is impossible in the sense in which it is impossible to have his sneeze. There are no states of affairs that would count as his feeling the same sensation as I do when I have pain, just as there are no states of affairs which would count as its being 5 o'clock in the afternoon on the sun. Since there is no criterion for determining the truth of the assertion 'He feels the same as I do when I have pain', the assertion is unintelligible.

Someone may still insist that though I am not able to specify the exact conditions yet I mean something when I say I can imagine your pain on the model of my own. To this Wittgenstein replies:

> the phrase 'I think I mean something by it', or 'I am sure, I mean something by it', which we so often hear in philosophical discussions to justify the use of an expression is for us no justification at all. We ask: 'What do you mean?', i.e., 'How do you use this expression?' If someone taught me the word 'bench' and said that *he sometimes* or always put a stroke over it thus: 'bench' and that this meant something to him. I should say: 'I do not know what sort of idea you associate with this stroke, but it does not interest me unless you show me that there is a use for

ably be no way in which anyone could learn the use of the word 'pain'.[16] So we have to agree that pain behaviour plays an indispensable part in the learning of the word 'pain'. By pain behaviour we mean the subject's reactions to certain forms of sensations.[17] For example, scratching is the typical reaction to an itch; a sharp cry and attention to the affected part often accompanies a certain kind of intense pain; and a different sort of vocal expression, like moaning, or a different sort of attention, like gentle rubbing of the affected part, constitute the typical behavioural responses to an ache. It is this general agreement in our shared pain behaviour — which in effect is a form of life — that renders the teaching and learning of sensation-language possible (cf. *PI* 241).

But someone may object here and say that even if there were no overt behaviour, you could teach a child the use of the word 'pain' by sticking a pin in his hand or by putting a flame under his hand, and telling him that this is what is called 'pain'. This method is called 'indirect ostensive teaching'. The objection, however, is not valid.

In the first place, in the absence of any overt behaviour on the part of the child, there is no guarantee that he felt anything, just as we do not have the idea of pain in the case of stones or plants. Wittgenstein expresses this idea in the following passage:

> What gives us *so much as the idea* that living beings, things, can feel?
> Is it that my education has led me to it by drawing my attention to feelings in myself, and now I transfer the idea to the objects outside myself? That I recognise that there is something there (in me) which I can call 'pain' without getting into conflict with the way other people use this word? — I do not transfer my idea to stones, plants, etc. Only of what behaves like a human being can one say that it *has* pains (*PI* 283).

In the second place there is no guarantee that he (the child) interprets our indirect ostensive definition correctly, that he does not take 'pain' to mean sticking a pin in his flesh, or damaging the flesh by putting a flame under his hand. One possible way for the elimination of these alternative interpretations of our ostensive definition is to tell him that it does not mean any overt action or state of affairs which everyone can observe, but that it only means the private sensation that he alone can feel. But this explanation is not enough. For, how can the child understand what we mean by 'sensation' and 'feeling'? Wittgenstein illustrates this point by taking the case in which a child is taught the name of a colour by an indirect method, that is, he is not taught the name of the colour by directly pointing at the colour but by making him see a white paper through different coloured spectacles. The different coloured spectacles are of different shapes. For instance, the red one is round, the green one elliptical, and so on. Now, there is no guarantee that he means by 'red' the round spectacles. Even if we tell him that 'red' is not the spectacles that he puts on his nose but the colour that he sees when he looks through it, it is quite clear that he will not be in a position to understand us, because he does not know what 'colour' means. So the whole act of this ostensive teaching does not make sense to a person who does not possess a language. (We shall discuss this point in detail a little later.)

Lastly, even if we suppose that he understands 'sensation' and 'feeling', how can we be sure that he feels the same sensation of pain when the pin is stuck into his hand? He may have felt only the piercing of the pin into his hand or something else.

All this, however, does not show that pain is not the name of a sensation; it only shows that the overt manifestations are a must for teaching or learning the word 'pain'. A child may see others groaning, crying, jerking their hands when they touch a hot plate, and claiming that it is painful. The child experiences what he himself feels when he touches hot things, or cries, or groans. In other words, the child learns that certain modes of behaviour are correlated with the inner sensations which are called pain. Thus, outward manifestations are necessary for a child to learn what pain is. He learns that pain is the sensation correlated with such overt manifestations, but that the overt manifestations are not identical with the pain or any part of it.

If 'pain' were the name of a sensation, then we could teach the use of 'pain' by an ostensive method, as we do in the case of names of physical objects, for example, in teaching 'fan', or physical properties, such as 'red'. The connection between the name of a public object, for example, 'tree', and the object which it denotes is established by certain modes of human behaviour, e.g., in pointing to the trees, in counting them, making pictures of them, planting them, and the like. None of these games can be played with the word 'pain'. For example, I cannot point to the pain (though I can point to the place of pain), nor can I show you pain (all I can show you is overt behaviour), nor draw a picture of pain. In fact, I can do practically nothing with the word 'pain' that I can do with the physical objects, colours, or shapes, in short with the publicly observable properties. Thus, none of the modes of human behaviour that constitutes the connection between the name of something and the thing named is available in the case of 'pain'. It follows then that 'pain' cannot be the name of a sensation.

Furthermore, the procedure of private ostensive definition, or mental ostentation, which on the private linguist's theory gives meaning to the words seems to be a possible procedure precisely because we do have the concepts of the object in question. For example, we do know what 'table' means, that it is a thing; or what 'red' means, that it is a colour. Therefore, when one gives us an ostensive definition of a certain concept, we understand (pick out) its meaning. Ostensive definition, as such, is a possible procedure for conveying or establishing the meaning of a word only for people already in possession of a language. The learner of a new language[18] is in a position to follow an ostensive definition, but the learner of an initial language[19] is not. In the case of 'pain' also, a private ostensive definition or subjective ostensive definition seems possible to us, because we do know what 'pain' means. We are under the illusion that one could always 'pick out' the sensation pain from the stream of one's consciousness and name it. But we forget that 'picking out' itself presupposes that we possess the concept of sensation, and therefore it cannot serve to explain our acquisition of it. A concept is not formed merely by looking at a thing, or a colour. To have a concept means to know how the word is used; it is to know the rules which govern the use of the word in the language game.

The foregoing discussion shows that if by 'pain' one means the word whose meaning is learnt by ostensive definition, then 'pain' is not the name of a sensation; and that private ostensive definition or mental ostentation cannot help a private linguist to acquire a concept. The only means available to him for acquiring a concept is private ostensive definition. But, acquisition of a concept, on the private linguist's theory, does not make any sense, with the result that a private language can never get started.

In the preceding section, we discussed the notion of concept acquisition. Let us suppose, for argument's sake, that a private linguist is somehow able to acquire a sensation-specifying concept.

We can ask him the question: Is it possible to retain the concept? By retention of a concept we mean using it correctly on future occasions. On the private linguist's theory, namely, that sensation specifying terms are names of sensations, possessing a concept is like having one mental filing cabinet in which examples are correlated with labels, that is, a name is put on each example for a sample of a sensation. The justification for using the 'name' again is its resemblance with the sample in the mental cabinet.

Now, a private linguist acquires a concept, say 'S', by a private ostensive definition. On his theory, there is no other way to acquire the concept. The question then arises, 'How shall he use the concept "S" on a future occasion?' — that is, 'How shall he know on a future occasion what he meant by "S"?' For, to apply the concept 'S' on a future occasion means that he must know the meaning of 'S'. But this is impossible in the private language. Wittgenstein says:

> Let us imagine a table (something like a dictionary) that exists only in our imagination. A dictionary can be used to justify the translation of a word X by a word Y. But are we also to call it a justification if such a table is to be looked up only in the imagination? — 'Well, yes; then it is a subjective justification' — But justification consists in appealing to something independent. — 'But surely I can appeal from one memory to another. For example I do not know if I have remembered the time of departure of a train right and to check it I call to mind how a page of the time table looked. Is not it the same here?' — No; for this process has got to produce a memory which is actually *correct*. If the mental image of the time table could not itself be tested for correctness, how could it confirm the correctness of the first memory? (As if someone were to buy several copies of the morning paper to assure himself that what it said was true.) Looking up a table in imagination is no more looking up a table than the image of the result of an imagined experiment is the result of an experiment (*PI* 265).

The only justification available to a private linguist for the use of 'S' on any occasion is his remembering the connection between 'S' and the object S. But, merely remembering the connection between a 'sign' and a 'sensation' does not always mean identifying the sensation correctly. But simply remembering which sensation the sign means and attaching meaning to a name does not mean acquiring infallibility in its use. For example, knowing what the word 'woman' means does not guarantee that one will never mistake a woman for a man, or knowing what 'toothache' means does not guarantee that one will never mistake a toothache for a gumache.

The justification, on a private linguist's theory, for using 'S' is his saying that it is 'S'. But, if having the same pain means the same as saying that one has the same pain then 'I have the same pain' means the same as 'I say I have the same pain' and the exclamation 'Oh!' means 'I say Oh!'[20]

The justification for using 'S', then, is a subjective justification. But the private linguist forgets that appealing for the justification of something is to ask for an objective criterion; otherwise, whatever I think is right shall be right. As Wittgenstein puts it: 'whatever is going to seem right to me is right. And that only means that here we cannot talk about "right"' (*PI* 258). In such circumstances not only is it impossible for the private linguist to identify a correct sign exampler, but it is also impossible for him to distinguish a correct from an incorrect correlation. He would not be able to use the word 'same', for he cannot distinguish between its correct and incorrect use.

One possible objection to this account can be that we do not generally ask for justification when we are engaged in our daily discourse. Then, why should we so much emphasise the requirement of justification in the case of a private language? In our day-to-day life, we do not consciously follow the rules, we do not first look at the rules and then make an assertion; we just develop habits of speech which rules describe. Thus, our following a rule is a matter of speech habit. From this, it follows that our use of 'same' in the day-to-day speech is a matter of habit. In the same way, a private linguist could also use the same word for something even if he did not know the rules governing the use of 'same'. He does not necessarily face any problem when he uses the word 'same' because he acts out of habit.[20]

This objection is invalid on two counts. In the first place, we are said to be in the habit of doing a thing only when we do the same thing regularly. For example, I am said to be having the habit of putting my hand on my nose whenever I speak only if people see me putting my hand on my nose whenever I speak to them. Now, I am said to have this habit only if someone has seen me putting my hand on my nose a number of times on the occasions on which I spoke to him or to anyone else. The criterion for anyone knowing whether I am in the habit of doing so is to see my hand on my nose on any occasion on which I speak. We can further illustrate this by taking another example. I am said to be in the habit of uttering 'No' after every sentence that I use in discourse with you only if people observed me doing this when I am engaged in talking with them. The criterion for knowing whether I am in the habit of saying 'No' after each sentence is to see me talking to people. If someone finds me consistently using the word 'No' after each sentence, then he can assume that I have this habit. So, doing a thing consistently culminates in what we call a habit. But a private linguist cannot use the same word for the same thing consistently, and hence cannot form the habit of using them.

In the second place, in case of doubt about the usage of a word in a public language where we habitually follow rules, we can always refer to the rules governing its use. Rules are something which are observed. Merely thinking that one is following or observing a rule is not observing it. Rules are objective and not subjective. A rule is not something which one follows once and once only in one's lifetime. It is what one does regularly. That is why we can always appeal to them for justification. It is because of their objective character that we are able to appeal to them when in doubt.

The notion of a 'private language' demands, however, that it must be possible to give oneself the 'private' rule: 'I will call the same thing "S" whenever it occurs.' But no objective check exists to determine what constitutes accord with this rule. A genuine rule must point towards the way in which it must be followed; but this 'private rule' does not point in any direction. Thus, the private linguist is the sole arbiter for deciding whether or not he has used the rule correctly, and no restrictions can be imposed on his application of the rule. The problem here has nothing whatsoever to do with the reliability of his memory. It is rather the question whether the very notion of remembering makes sense in the context of his 'private language'. If he doubts his memory, then he can look for a confirmation. But, confirmation makes sense only in the case of public language and not in the case of private language. There can be neither a question of confirmation nor of doubt in the case of private language. For, there is just no rule for what is the same and what is not the same; there is no distinction between correct and incorrect. It is for this reason that what the private linguist says does not make any difference. And, this implies that he does not say anything; because if he said anything, it should make a difference.

A private linguist may say that 'I speak or write the sign down, and at the same time I concentrate my attention on the sensation ... in this way I impress on myself the connection between the sign and the sensation' (*PI* 258). Thus impressing, or concentrating one's attention on the sensation that accompanies when he wishes to say 'S' may be another justification offered by a private linguist for his use of 'S'. For example, whenever he uses the word 'S' he has a particular sensation, and it is this particular sensation 'in' him which makes him say 'S'. He may say that 'The occurrence of this sensation is the justification for my using "S".' To this Wittgenstein's reply is: 'The very fact that we should so much like to say: "*This* is the important thing" — while we point privately to the sensation — is enough to show how much we are inclined to say something which gives no information' (*PI* 298).

A third alternative is that a private linguist correlates his use of 'S' with a publicly observable phenomenon. Consider the following example of Wittgenstein's:

> Let us now imagine a use for the entry of the sign 'S' in my diary. I discover that whenever I have a particular sensation a manometer shows that my blood-pressure rises. So I shall be able to say that my blood-pressure is rising without using any apparatus. This is a useful result. And now it seems quite indifferent whether I have recognised the sensation *right* or not. Let us suppose I regularly identify it wrong, it does not matter in the least, and that alone shows that the hypothesis that I make a mistake is mere show. (We as it were turned a knob which looked as if it could be used to turn on some part of the machine; but it was a mere ornament, not connected with the mechanism at all) (*PI* 270).

In this case, there is a check on my use of 'S', namely, seeing that whenever I used 'S', my blood pressure rises. To see whether I remember the meaning of 'S' right I do not have merely to rely on my memory but can check it up by seeing the mercury rising in the manometer. Here, then, 'S' has a genuine use, but not as a part of private language, because in private language any person other than the speaker cannot know that the speaker is having a sensation. But in such a situation, 'S' is tantamount to a 'sensation which means my blood pressure is rising'. If the private linguist tries to justify his use of 'S' by associating it with a public referent, then 'S' is not a word in a private language; but it is a word that is tantamount to a sensation which means 'so and so', a public referent.

We have shown that the only means for a private linguist to justify his use of 'S' is to appeal to his memory. But, as we have discussed above, memory alone is not a sufficient criterion for our consistent use of 'S'. From this, it follows that there is no way in which he could consistently use 'S'. It seems, then, that on his theory, any assertion, if at all it is possible to make one, would have to perform two functions simultaneously. One: it must perform the function of a statement, and two: it must at the same time serve as a definition, in that the speaker shall have to specify the meaning of 'S' every time he uses it. But this is impossible; for making a statement and giving a definition are two different speech acts. They cannot simultaneously be combined in one and the same act of asserting. Thus, on the private linguist's theory, even retention of a concept does not make sense. It follows then that even if, *per impossible*, a private language could ever get started, it could never persist.

I close this chapter with two remarks:
One: The assumption that a private language is possible leads to the consequence that a language could be invented; for, the notion of a private language involves that each one of us invents a new language to report on his inner experiences. But this is absurd, because inventing a new language (in the sense that it involves inventing new 'form of life') is impossible. To invent a language means to invent a new way of following rules, making promises, giving orders, and so on. All these presuppose usages, practices, conventions, rules and a host of other similar things. To invent a new language thus means to invent a new 'form of life'. Nobody would dispute the fact that a form of life cannot be invented but is evolved. Therefore, the supposition that a private language can be invented is false. Hence, private language is impossible.
Two: Wittgenstein wanted to show not only that 'private language' is impossible, but also that those who hold the view that a language can be private, or that 'private language' is possible, are making a category mistake. They ignore the social nature of language. A language is a set of activities, or practices defined by certain rules which govern the various uses of the words in the language. In

short, language is a 'form of life'. As Wittgenstein says: 'to imagine a language is to imagine a form of life' (*PI* 23); [Language] is not agreement in opinion but is a form of life' (*PI* 24); and 'that the speaking of a language is part of the activity or of a form of life' (*PI* 23). Nobody would dispute the assertion 'that a "form of life" cannot be private'. For, 'private' is not a concept which can be used with the concept 'form of life'. Those who allocate the concept 'private' to the concept 'language' have thus made a category mistake.

Notes

1. Cf. O.R. Jones (ed.), *Private Language Argument*, London: Macmillan, 1970, Introduction.
2. Translated by G.E.M. Anscombe, Oxford: Basil Blackwell, 1968, third edition, henceforth to be referred to as 'PI'.
3. It may appear, from this, as if there can be private rules in a private language. But I shall argue in the course of this chapter that there cannot possibly be rules which are followed privately; for the expression 'private rule' itself involves a category mistake.
4. London: George Allen and Unwin, 1934.
5. Ibid., p. 80.
6. Cf. Anthony Kenny, *Wittgenstein*, Allan Lane (1973), p. 185.
7. Cf. Anthony Manser, 'Pain and Private Language', *Studies in the Philosophy of Wittgenstein*, ed. Peter Winch, London: Routledge and Kegan Paul (1969), pp. 166-84.
8. L. Wittgenstein, *On Certainty*, ed. by G.E.M. Anscombe and G.H. von Wright, translated by Dennis Paul and G.E.M. Anscombe, New York and Evanston: J. & J. Harper Edition, 1969, henceforth to be referred to as 'OC', 58.
9. *The Blue and Brown Books*, Oxford: Basil Blackwell, 1960 (hereafter 'BB'), p. 69.
10. *Zettle*, Oxford: Basil Blackwell, 1947 (hereafter 'Z'), p. 571.
11. G.E. Moore, 'Wittgenstein's Lectures in 1930-33', *Philosophical Papers*, London: George Allen and Unwin, 1959, pp. 273-4.
12. *The Problem of Knowledge*, Harmondsworth: Penguin Books, 1956.
13. L. Wittgenstein, 'Private Experience', ed. Rush Rhees, *Philosophical Review*, LXXVII, 1968, p. 314.
14. 'I want to keep a diary about the recurrence of a certain sensation. To this end I associate it with the sign "S" and write the sign in a calendar for every day on which I have a sensation. — I will remark first of all that a definition of the sign cannot be formulated.— But still I can give myself a kind of ostensive definition. — How? Can I point to the sensation? Not in the ordinary sense. — But I speak, or write the sign down, and at the same time concentrate my attention on the sensation. — And so, as it were, point it inwardly' (*PI* 258).
15. L. Wittgenstein, 'Private Experience'.
16. 'What would it be like if human beings showed no outward signs of pain (did not groan, grimace, etc.). Then it would be impossible to teach a child the word "toothache" (*PI* 125).

17. This includes not only the present short-term bodily behaviour, but also the future and past behaviour.
18. By learning a new language is meant learning another language. For example, if I already know English and start learning French, then I shall be said to be learning a new language.
19. But if I do not know any language, then I shall be said to be learning the initial language. For example, a child when he learns his mother tongue is said to be learning the initial language.
20. Cf. L. Wittgenstein, 'Private Experience'.
21. Cf. W. Todd, 'Wittgenstein on Private Language', *Philosophical Quarterly*, 12 (1962).

3   SELF-KNOWLEDGE AND PERSONAL IDENTITY

So far, we have maintained that 'sensations' are neither private (Chapter 1) nor do we need a private language to express them (Chapter 2). In this chapter, I utilise these conclusions to show that self-knowledge, or the knowledge of one's own mind, is attained neither by introspection, nor through any other 'method' to which the owner has a privileged access, but that it is gained by and through the knowledge of the world, or the total form of life. In this respect I have sharply departed from Ryle's view that one knows about one's own self, or mind, by observing one's own behaviour and the like. To establish my thesis that one does not use any criterion to know about one's own mind, or self, I have done two things:

One: I have examined and rejected some of the major theories about the nature of mind and connected with it the introspection theory of self-knowledge.

Two: I have discussed the nature of personal identity. In the main I have rejected the theories advocating the memory and bodily criteria of personal identity respectively. I have argued for the thesis that we need not have any special theories to account for first person personal identity judgements; one who considers that self-knowledge and personal identity present a problem is mistaken, for he fails to recognise that it is a basic feature of our life that we know about ourselves and about our identity without any theories.

Alice in *Alice's Adventures in Wonderland* says at one place, 'Who in the world am I? Ah!, that is a great puzzle'. Philosophers have tried to find a solution to this puzzle. In our day-to-day discourse, one is apt to answer the question 'What or who am I?' by one or all of the following: 'I am X', 'I am the son of Y', 'I am an Indian', 'I am an amateur musician', 'I am a taxpayer', 'I am a philosopher', and the like. But, when a philosopher asks this question (in his professional moments) he does not ask what things I happen to be, but what I essentially am. In other words, he is interested in what 'I' essentially refers to. What gives rise to the belief that 'I' must refer to something is the use of the word 'I' as a grammatical subject in first person psychological statements. 'We say "I think so and so" and this word "I" suggests that thinking is the act of a person.[1] The basis of the idea that 'I' refers to something does not lie so much in the fact that the word 'I' functions, grammatically, as a subject as in the fact that corresponding to any first person statement there are third person statements that are in a certain sense equivalent to it and certainly are about something. For example, X's saying 'I have a toothache' is equivalent to Y's saying 'X has a toothache.' Since these third person statements are certainly about persons, or selves, the first person statements must also be about persons, or selves. Thus, the word 'I' must refer to a person, or a self. The question 'What am I?' is therefore equivalent to the question 'What is a person?' or 'What is a self?' So if I can discover what I am, then I shall also know what sort of a thing a person or a self is?[2]

The word 'I' sometimes is used to refer to my body as in the case of 'I am writing', 'I am six-foot tall', or 'I have a fair complexion.' In all these cases the word 'I' can be replaced by 'my body'. Similarly, there are cases in which 'I' refers to the mechanical auxiliaries to the body, as for example, in 'I am out of gas', or 'I collided with a pillar box', the word 'I' stands not for my body but for the car in which I am or was travelling. 'So sometimes we can, and sometimes we cannot, paraphrase the first person pronoun by "my body"[3]. Now, in the statements 'I am out of gas' or 'I collided with a pillar box', the word 'I' does not refer to myself, rather it is an abbreviation for something that belongs to me, namely my car. Similarly, 'I' in the statements 'I am six-foot tall', or 'I am writing', or 'I have a fair complexion' is an abbreviation for 'my body' which in some way belongs to me and is not really I, or the self. There is another set of statements which we have called 'first person psychological statements', for example, 'I have toothache', 'I am depressed', 'I am annoyed', and 'I am thinking', in which the word 'I' does not refer to my body. The fact that the word 'I' in these statements does not refer to 'my body' is demonstrated by the fact that the word 'I' in them cannot be replaced by the words 'my body'. For, if we do so, we shall be in the absurd position of saying that my body is depressed, or that my body is annoyed. Moreover, one can know the truth of these first person psychological statements without knowing anything about one's body. From this it appears that the word 'I' in all these statements is the subject of experience, and that this word necessarily refers to a person or a self. Of all the first person statements, therefore, it is the first person psychological statements that refer to persons who are thinking, intelligent beings, having reason and reflection.[4] Here we are getting closer to Descartes' *Cogito* argument. He argued, for example, that he could doubt the existence of bodies, but that he could not himself be a body. However, the fact that one can know some truths about oneself without knowing any facts about one's body does not lead to the Cartesian conclusion that a person could exist without having physical properties. All it leads to is that some facts about a person are not facts about his body, or, in other words, some properties of a person are not physical properties.

From the preceding discussion, it follows that 'I' does not necessarily refer to a body, but that it refers to a being to which first person psychological statements, namely, 'I have toothache', 'I believe that it will rain' and the like can be ascribed. In other words, 'I' necessarily refers to a being that experiences, thinks, desires, wills, and so on. This is what Descartes had in mind when he said 'What then am I? A conscious being. What is that? A being that doubts, understands, asserts, is willing, is unwilling; further, that has sense and imagination'.[5] Thomas Reid also had the same thing in mind when he replied to a similar question by saying: 'Whatever the self may be, it is something which thinks, and deliberates, and resolves, and acts, and suffers'.[6] Now, doubting, understanding, asserting, willing, suffering and thinking are psychological features, and psychological features can be ascribed only to a being which is characterised by mind. Therefore, 'I' necessarily refers to a being characterised by mind. We have already said that 'I' essentially refers to a person.[7] Therefore, a person or a self essentially is characterised by a mind.

The question 'What am I?' is, therefore, equivalent to the question 'What is a self?' or 'What is a mind?' The question 'What is a self?' or 'What is a mind?' is an enquiry into the nature of self, or mind. In a discussion on this topic, the expression 'substance', 'pure ego' and 'subject' are regarded as synonymous. The term 'pure ego' is defined by Broad as meaning 'a particular existent which is of a different kind from any event; it owns events but is not itself an event'.[8] Russell defined 'subject' as meaning 'any entity which is acquainted with something'.[9] In the history of philosophy, this discussion is centred on the question 'Is self or mind a substance?'

Though Plato and St Augustine talked of mind as something distinct from body, Descartes was the first philosopher in the

Western world to develop and propound the nature of mind. For him, mind is an enduring, immaterial, non-extended substance whose essential nature is thought. By 'thought' he meant acts of doubting, understanding, conceiving, affirming, denying, willing, referring, imagining, and feeling.[10] The claim that a self or mind is a substance is sometimes expressed by saying that it is a subject of thought and experience. Thomas Reid expressed his contention that mind is a substance by saying: 'I am not thought, I am not action, I am not feeling; I am something that thinks, and acts, and suffers'.[11] In this view, the states and acts of a self or mind are the states and acts of which it is necessarily aware. Furthermore, this awareness is incapable of being deceptive. These acts and states, by definition, are such that their occurrence entails that they are known to the mind of which they are acts and states. In other words, they are, by definition, self-intimating. It is held, on those theories, that mind can 'see' or 'look at' its own states and acts in the light emitted by itself. This capacity of the mind is sometimes conveyed by using such other expressions as 'over hearing' 'phosphorescence', 'self luminousness', 'refulgent', 'conscious', and their stylistic variants. A mind, on this view, is conscious of its states not in the sense that one could report on them *post mortem* but in the sense that its consciousness goes along with its happening as if it were co-axial with it.[12] The report on the deliverances from this consciousness would be in the present tense. Moreover, I am conscious of my mental states not in the sense that I could, if I liked, tell someone what I was experiencing or thinking, but that I am conscious of my mental acts and states in the sense that I am actively cognisant of them, that at every moment I know the mental state in which I am at that particular moment. On this view, therefore, if I think, doubt, understand, will, imagine, regret, or feel pain, then I know *ipso facto* that I am thinking, doubting, understanding, willing, feeling pain.

I propose now to show that, irrespective of the truth or falsity of the doctrine that mind is a substance, the above account of self-knowledge given by its supporters is wrong. First, if we were conscious of all the mental acts, then we could never hold certain things to be true which are in fact false. For example, we are sometimes not conscious of the fact that we are dreaming when we are dreaming; and conversely, we are sometimes not aware that we are not dreaming when we are awake. Similarly, we are sometimes not conscious that we are irritated, excited, annoyed, or frustrated.

person can have self-knowledge, or knowledge of his mental states, by observing these perceptions. Since these 'perceptions' are being attentively and deliberately scrutinised, they are the objects of observation. Further this 'observation' is not carried out by any of our sense organs; so it is non-sensuous and is technically called introspection. Introspection differs from outer observation in the following respects:

(a) The objects of observation are in principle observable by any suitably placed observer, whereas the objects of introspection can be introspected only by the one whose states they are, and by no one else.

(b) Observation involves functioning of a bodily organ, whereas introspection does not.

(c) Observation can be wrong; but introspection is veridical; it cannot be wrong. Its reports are incorrigible.

Introspection differs from consciousness in that introspection is an attentive operation which is occasionally performed to find out what is going on in our mind, while consciousness is an essential element of all the mental acts and states, and it is a constant as distinguished from occasional function of the mind.[19]

Introspection also differs from retrospection in that introspection is the inner observation of a present state, or act of mind, whereas retrospection is the action of looking back at a past state, or act of mind. Retrospection is a review of past events, or conditions.

I shall now try to show that the view that we know the acts and states of our mind by introspection is untenable. My reasoning is as follows.

Firstly, if my knowing a mental act or state — say, my being in pain — involves introspection, then I must inwardly inspect or perceive (this is what we mean by introspection) something; for introspection requires both an object and a subject. It seems natural to answer the question 'What do I perceive when I have a pain?' by saying 'The pain.' But, this is an absurd answer; it leads us to another question 'What do I perceive when I perceive a pain?' Obviously, there is no answer that can be given to such a question. But on the introspection theory, even in such cases, there must be something that I perceive or introspect.

Secondly, on this theory, the observer has to perform two

actions at the same time. One to do the action, and the other, to know by introspection that he is doing it. 'He would, for example, be both resolving to get up early and concomitantly observing his act of resolving; attending to the programme of rising betimes and perceptually attending to his programme'.[20] But this again leads us to an infinite regression. For, the only answer available on this theory to the question 'How do you know that you have resolved to get up early in the morning?' is 'I know it from introspection.' But this answer invites another question: 'How do you know that you know it from introspection?' The only answer available to a theorist is 'From another act of introspection.' This chain shall continue *ad infinitum*. An introspection theorist may say here that it is not a synchronous act of attention to both the actions, but is a rapid to and fro switch-over of attention from one act to the other. While saying this he forgets that if introspection is so described then there is a time lag, however small, between the mental state and its observation. But this was not the original definition of introspection; rather it was of retrospection. There is no dispute over the fact that many states of mind can only be examined in retrospect. While introspection involves privileged access, retrospection does not. Our observation, therefore, is that introspection does not provide us with adequate account of self-knowledge.

The fact that the 'substance theory' and the 'bundle theory' of the self give absurd accounts of self-knowledge is a sufficient ground for rejecting both of them. The underlying assumptions of these theories which lead them to give an absurd account of self-knowledge are as follows:

Both these theories are based on the assumption that all mental happenings are ghostly episodes, which are the work of a ghost, namely, the mind, whose home is in the body. On the substance theory, the reflective observer was encouraged to think of himself, of his palpable bodily self, as inhabited by a ghost, or rather as being that ghost. And, the introspection theory was raised to tell us about the way in which the ghost is supposed to directly observe himself and his acts and states as contrasted with the way in which he observes the outside world through the mediacy of the body it inhabits. This basic assumption of the two theorists, however, is wrong, for when we talk of a person's mind, we do not talk of a ghost in the body, or a self-luminous substance, or a theatre of special status incidents, but of certain ways in which some of the (psychic) incidents of his life are ordered. ' "Mind" is not the name of another person, working or frolicking behind an impenetrable screen: it is not the name of another place where work is done or games are played: and it is not the name of another tool with which work is done, or another appliance with which games are played.'[21] Mind is not a thing or a substance or a theatre which exists independently as other material objects exist. A mind exists in so far and only in so far as one or more of a person's mental capacities are being expressed. The term 'capacity' used here is synonymous with capability, power, ability, faculty and disposition of willing, hoping, feeling, imagining, acting, perceiving, remembering, thinking, deciding, wishing, hating, fearing, regretting and so on. All these acts are called mental acts and the words that express these mental acts are called mental concepts. Mind is attributed to a being, capable of performing mental acts. From this it follows that the characteristic of possessing a mind is attributable only to a being to whom mental concepts are applicable. The existence of a mind, therefore, is inferred from mental concepts alone. Hence only mental concepts are the constituents of a mind. Apart from these concepts, a mind cannot be conceived. Mind, in other words, is a complex of concepts. It is one term for all these concepts. We may call it a blanket concept which envelops thinking, willing, feeling, hoping, fearing, or in short all the mental concepts. It follows from this that a mind does not exist alongside or besides these concepts but that it is something that is embedded both individually and collectively in them. This special feature can be illustrated by taking the example of the British Constitution. It is also a blanket concept which envelops the civil service, the judiciary, the established church, the House of Commons, the House of Lords and the Royal Family. Clearly, the British Constitution is not something that exists alongside or beside all of them, but its existence is implied by one, or all of them.

A person's life is not a double series of events taking place in two different kinds of stuff, physical and mental; rather, 'It is one concatenation of events, the difference between some and other classes of which largely consists in its applicability or inapplicability to them of logically different types of law-propositions and law-like propositions'.[22]

Assertions about a person's mind are assertions of a special sort about that person. Their speciality consists in the fact that they are not about any particular organ, but, that *they are not about any organ at all.* The mistake of the theorists in thinking of mind as an organ lies in their thinking that the statements of the form 'His mind thinks, chooses, feels, or knows' make logically sound statements. Their mistake lies in not realising that 'It is a logical solecism to speak ... of someone's mind knowing this, or choosing that. The person himself knows this or chooses that, though the fact that he does so can, if desired, be classified as a mental fact about that person. In partly the same way it is improper to speak of my eyes seeing this, or my nose smelling that; we should say, rather, that I see this, or I smell that, and that these assertions carry with them certain facts about my eyes and nose. But this analogy is not exact, for while my eyes and nose are organs of sense, 'my mind' does not stand for another organ. It signifies my ability and proneness to do certain things and not some piece of personal apparatus without which I could or would not do them'.[23] And the questions about the relation between a person and his mind, like those about the relation between a person's body and his mind, are improper questions. They are improper in much the same way as is the question, 'What transactions go on between the House of Commons and the British Constitution?'[24] In our view, therefore, the concept of a person is a primary concept. By saying that the concept of a person is a primary concept we mean

> the concept of a person is not to be analysed as that of an animated body or of an embodied anima. This is not to say that the concept of a pure individual consciousness might not have a logically secondary existence, if one thinks, or finds, it desirable. We speak of a dead person as a body and in the same secondary way we might at best think of a disembodied person, retaining the logical benefit of individuality from having been a person'.[25]

But in all our ordinary discourse, 'mind' is given directly with the bodily presence. The mental is intermingled with what is done. Mind *per se* cannot be isolated; a man's mental slackness appears from his demeanour and conduct, just as the acumen of the chess champion becomes apparent from his moves.

Within the framework of this or that scientific discipline it is, of course, possible to adopt a particular viewpoint and to discuss only the physical, or the psychical; but the datum referred to is in reality the same. The situation is comparable to the case of a flock of birds flying southwards, which can be a case of bird migration or it may only be that a number of birds are flying southwards. For the biologist it makes a big difference one way or the other; but from the physicist's point of view, the migration and the flying towards the south are one and the same datum.[26] Similarly, mind is not mysterious something, something 'besides' what is given any more than a bird migration is something besides or something other than the observation of a flying of a flock of birds towards the south. Nor is mind a mysterious something that accompanies a mental concept. In ordinary language, when we talk of a mental concept being accompanied by mind, the word 'accompany' is used in a sense in which a lone traveller can be accompanied by my good wishes.

To repeat, surface similarity between the expressions 'my nose', 'my ears', 'my eyes', 'my hands' and the expressions 'my mind', 'A healthy mind in a healthy body', 'The relation between mind and matter', 'Why does the mind have a body?' has led many philosophers to think of mind as a special organ of sense. So, the first mistake of the theorists, namely, that mind is an organ, had its basis in not realising that this analogy is misleading, for 'my mind' does not stand for any organ; rather it signifies my ability and proneness to do certain things, and not some piece of personal apparatus without which I could or would not do them. Mind is a more or less well integrated set of capacities. Clearly, on this view, the question 'What knowledge can a person get of the workings of his own mind?', or the question 'How does one get it?', by their wordings, are absurd and senseless questions. For they suppose 'mind' to be an organ, or a demon that works inside a person's body, which in fact it is not. These questions are excluded from the language games played with 'mind'.

From what we have said so far, it follows that the question 'How do I know that I have a mind?' breaks up into several sub-questions such as 'How do I know that I have pain?', 'How do I know that I am afraid?', 'How do I know that I am sad?', 'How do I know that I am in love?', and so on. The second mistake of the theorists had its basis in their belief that all first person psychological statements must be made on some evidence. My being acquainted with 'this evidence' must be a reason or basis for asserting 'this psychological assertion'. They thought that these questions are requests for the criterion for asserting such first person present tense psychological statements as 'I am in pain' 'I am sad', 'I am happy', and the like. Accordingly, they sought to find out criteria for asserting them. Since these assertions cannot be inferred from anything including bodily behaviour, they thought that these must be based on some non-physical fact, namely, my peeping into a windowless chamber to which I have a privileged access. Alternatively, the fact of my being conscious of pain must be my criterion or my ground for asserting 'I am in pain.' We have already shown in our discussion on privacy and private language that the question 'How do I know that I am in pain?' is a senseless question. We have also shown in the course of this chapter that there is no such windowless chamber called mind to which we have privileged access. So, the question of my peeping into such a chamber does not arise; nor can it serve as a criterion for my saying 'I am in pain.'

So far we have not considered the view that the criterion or the justification for my saying 'I am in pain' is my being acquainted or being directly aware of the pain itself, or just the fact of my being in pain. My criterion is therefore a private one. This view is mistaken. Because, first pain is not an entity and on this view pain has to be an entity of which one can be aware. Second:

> if being aware of a pain were observing a pain and therefore involved being in such a position, it would have to be the case that it can be an open question, to be settled empirically, whether a person who is in pain and thinks that he is in pain is in fact aware of a pain; that it is possible for a person to be in pain without being aware of pain; and that being aware of a pain is one of several possible ways of knowing that one is in pain. But none of these things is the case.[27]

Thirdly, if the only possible reason for saying 'I am in pain' were 'I am aware of pain' and this reason is always correct then it is no criterion at all. For if a question has one answer only such that that answer is always correct, then the question to which this is the answer is a pointless question.[28]

The belief that the first person psychological statements are based on some evidence, which is the reason for asserting them, is mistaken. It rests on a conceptual confusion of treating 'pain' as the name of an entity.[29] To the question 'How do I know that this colour is red?' the only answer available is: 'I have learnt English'.[30] Similarly, the criterion for asserting a first person psychological statement is our knowing the language in which it is expressed. We do not have to look for any other reason, nor is there one. This in fact is true not only in the case of the first person psychological statements, but it is true also in the case of other statements such as 'This is a tree', 'This is an inkpot' when made under such circumstances as it would be absurd for us to express this with hesitation or reservation. In all such cases although what I say is based on sense experience it is not known by any sort of inference. I do not have any evidence for what I say, and I could not, now, think of any evidence against it. If we still insist on finding out some reason for asserting such statements, then 'my reason will soon give out. And then I shall act without reasons' (*PI* 211). We do not need any justification, proof, or guarantee which the theorist thought we must have for asserting first person psychological statements. We are not less rational for managing our lives without them. In this respect I sharply disagree with Ryle who holds that one knows about one's own mind in much the same way in which one knows about other minds.[31] 'Our knowledge of other people and of ourselves depends upon noticing how they and we behave'. On his view, therefore, the assertions 'I am in pain', 'I am sad', or 'I am happy', and the like need some justification. This justification may consist in observing the bodily behaviour. But this is absurd; for we do not assert first person psychological statements after observing our bodies. I agree with Wittgenstein and hold that such psychological states as being in pain, being sad and being happy are the formal features of our lives, and the first person expressions embodying them such as 'I am in pain', 'I am sad', 'I am happy' do not need any reasoning. They are simply the ways in which I act (cf. *PI* 217). 'It is natural for us to say a sentence in such and such surroundings, and unnatural for us to say it in isolation' (*PI* 595). The whole idea of proof, or justification or reasoning about formal features of our life is a confused one.

The third mistake of the theorists consisted in assuming that all thinking, believing, feeling, and the like must take place in the mind. This led them to attribute a substantival or a 'theatrical' character to the mind. But this assumption, namely, that all thinking, believing, or feeling must take place in the mind, is wrong. For thinking does not take place in a place called mind, but it takes place on the paper on which I write, or on the work of art which I create. In short, my thinking, or feeling is manifested in my actions. This is supported by the fact that in our day-to-day life, we speak about a person's character being evidenced by his actions, or a genius being manifested in a piece of sculpture. Similarly, the mind is not something permanently curtained off; but we detect it in the studio, at the workbench, or on the chess board, or in the innumerable other conditions.

The fourth, and the most crucial, mistake of the theorists consisted in thinking of 'I' as a thing among things. Since they could not find any observable thing to which 'I' refers, they thought that it must refer to a mysterious something, to which they gave the name 'Mind'. Their mistake consisted in thinking that 'I' has a stable referent. It is a mistake, because 'I' does not have a stable referent. ' "I" indicates the person who utters it'.[32] In my use of 'I' it always indicates me and only me. In your use of it, it indicates you and only you. In his use of it, it refers always to him and only him. 'I' does not have a stable, but a shifting referent. As 'I' does not have a stable but a shifting referent, it can, therefore, be called an 'index word'. Ryle likens it in this respect to a word such as 'now' which also can be applied to any point whatever in the time series.[33] Wittgenstein expresses the same fact by saying that 'I' is not the name of a person, nor 'here' of a place, and 'this' is not a name (*PI* 410).

From all the discussion so far, it follows that 'I' is not the name of mysterious, concealed substance. The 'I' has a meaning and location within the contingencies of everyday experience. That is, 'I' turns up along with the world in concrete living. This 'I' can never be netted as an object because it is exhibited as I in company with events and things as they ordinarily occur. For knowing 'I' we do not have to posit any 'private world'. It reveals itself in the public, objective world; rather it is coexistent with it. It is not something hidden away, as the theorists assumed; but is something that is continually being manifested neither as an object, nor as a little 'world', but as something that accompanies the world. One cannot know 'I' or mind or self in isolation from the world. On the contrary, one knows it when one knows about the world. In other words, self-knowledge begins when one has contacts with the world and not before.

The question 'What or who am I?' besides asking 'What kind of a person am I?', or 'What is my essential nature?' also asks 'What particular person am I?', or 'In what sense am I the same person who slept last night, or who was born twenty-five years ago, etc.?', or 'What is it that makes a set of experiences, or descriptions which are logically independent of one another into the description of one and the same person, namely, myself?' Or, as Russell put it: 'Why do we regard our present and past experiences as all parts of one experience, namely the experience we call "ours"?'[34] All these questions are requests for the criteria of personal identity. The word 'identity' is not used here in the sense in which it is used in the statements 'The Morning star is the same as the Evening star', or 'The lightning flash you saw is the same as the one I saw.' Here, it is used in a sense in which it implies persistence, or to use Hume's term the 'continuance', that is, the existence of one and the same thing at different times. And by identity judgements or identity statements are meant judgements, or statements, that are expressible in sentences of the form 'X existing at t_1, is the same as Y existing at t_2 where t_1 and t_2 refer to different times.'

It almost seems a contradiction to say 'X at 2 and X at 52 is the same person' because they are so different. How are we to account for the unity we assume people to have throughout their lives? This is precisely the problem of personal identity. It is the problem of clarifying the principles underlying the process of reidentification or recognising persons. To reidentify or to recognise someone is to say or imply that, despite the lapse of time and the changes it may have wrought, the person before me now is the same as the person I knew before. Penelhum describes the problem of personal identity 'as that of trying to justify a practice which seems at first sight strange, and even paradoxical. This is the practice of talking about people as single beings in spite of the fact that they are constantly changing, and over a period of time may have changed completely'.[35] The criteria that we offer for personal identity in particular and identity in general have not only to be criteria of individuating, that is, differentiating one person, or one thing from another co-existing person, or thing, but also the criteria for knowing what is it which warrants the belief that it is the same individual that has persisted over a stretch of time. These criteria have to be logically necessary and sufficient conditions of identity.

Different things have different criteria of identity. The nature of a particular class of things helps us in determining the criteria of identity for them. (For example, in the case of material things, such as tables, chairs, and stones, we can treat spatio-temporal continuity as a criterion of their identity.) As Strawson puts it: 'One of the requirements for the identity of a material thing is that its existence, as well as being continuous in time, should be continuous in space'.[36] But in the case of other entities such as regiments, teams, and corporations, spatio-temporal continuity obviously cannot be the criterion of their identity. Conversely, the criterion that we use in making judgements about the identity of objects, or entities of a certain kind reflects on the nature of that sort of object or entity. It follows that the criterion which we use for personal identity depends much on the nature of persons.

Earlier in this chapter we said that the essential nature of persons is characterised by the fact that they have minds. It is for this reason that the theorists equated the question 'In what does the identity of a person consist?' with the question 'In what does the identity of a mind consist?' We have already shown there (a) that it makes no sense to say that the mind is a substance, and (b) that the philosophers have a tendency to regard minds as non-physical entities. Their belief that mind is a non-physical entity presents the theorists with a special problem about personal identity for two reasons. These are:

(i) The question of personal identity cannot be decided by merely deciding the identity of a body. For one thing, mind by its very nature is distinct from the body. For another, one can make identity judgements about oneself and know them to be true without first knowing the facts about one's body. Lastly, if identity consisted in the continuance of the body, then the answer to the question 'What is the criterion for saying that "these" experiences are mine?' will be that they are the experiences which are causally dependent upon the state of my body. But the proposition that all of my experiences are causally dependent upon the state of my body is analytic; it is just a way of saying that all the experiences which are causally dependent upon the state of my body are causally dependent upon the state of my body.

(ii) The second reason is self-consciousness. It concerns the fact that there is a peculiar sense in which a person is conscious of his own identity. This is the sense in which persons make identity judgements about themselves without having, or needing, the sort of evidence we use in making identity judgements about persons other than ourselves, that is, they face a problem of justifying their beliefs in other selves.

Let us now search for the criteria that we use in making identity judgements about ourselves. We want in other words to find out the criterion of first person personal identity. From the discussion above, one is easily led to the conclusion that the real criterion of first person identity cannot be bodily or physical criterion but that it must be some psychological or mental criterion that one has to know to be satisfied in one's own case without knowing anything about one's body. One knows one's thoughts, feelings, and images without knowing anything about one's body, but none of them can be regarded as the criterion of personal identity. For all of them are far less stable than the body; and it is not easy to find out what Hume calls 'the bond that unites them'. However, the case of memory is different.

One does not have to observe or know anything about one's body to make past tense statements about oneself on the basis of memory, yet these statements, grounded directly in one's memory, imply the persistence of the person whose memories they are. Locke was the originator of the view that memory is the only source of our own identities. He says, apparently to define personal identity, that 'whatever has the consciousness of present and past actions is the same person to whom they both belong'.[37] By 'consciousness' he means here both an awareness of what one is doing when one is doing it and an ability to remember having done it. The view that memory is the criterion of personal identity is commonly held by all the bundle theorists. H.P. Grice expressed it by saying 'the self is a logical construction, and is to be defined in terms of memory'.[38] Russell said: 'A total group of my experiences throughout time may be defined in terms of memory',[39] and 'What we know is this string of experiences that make up a person, and that is put together by means of certain relations, such, for example, as memory'.[40] According to Hume, 'the memory not only discovers the identity [of a person], but also contributes to its production by producing the relations of resemblance among the perceptions'.[41] Ayer held that there are criteria of personal identity which

> may be called the psychological criteria of continuity of disposition and memory. We may say that a series of experiences constitutes the history of a single person, if similar mental states recur throughout the series in similar conditions, and if as the series is prolonged, its later sections always contain some

experiences that are memories of the earlier'.[42]

D. Wiggins also argues that memory is a criterion of personal identity.[43]

These memory theorists claim that in memory we have a special, logically distinct, access to our own identities, and that without such access to our own identities the very notion of a person would be inapplicable. As Shoemaker says,

> Each of us has in memory, a kind of access to his own past history which no other than himself can have. The statements we make about our own past histories are not infallible but they are immune to one sort of error to which statements of other persons about our past histories are subject; they are immune to what might be called error through misidentification'.[44]

This amounts to saying that if I make a statement 'I broke the front window yesterday' and if my statement is based on memory, and also if my memory is accurate, then it is impossible that I should be mistaken as to whether it was I who did it. On the other hand, if I say on the basis of memory that 'That is the man who stole my watch', I could be mistaken as to the identity of the man even though my memory is accurate; for the man in front of me may be his twin.

Their reason for holding memory to be a criterion of personal identity is another related fact about it. The fact, in Shoemaker's words is this: 'If a person remembers any event at all, whether it be an action of his own, an action of another person, or an event that is not the action of anyone it follows that he, the very person who remembers, must have witnessed the event at the time of its occurrence'.[45] This way of putting the causal nature of memory, however, is not completely accurate. For, one can remember one's own actions, and it is normally not the case that one observes or witnesses one's action, while performing them. It seems more accurate to say that if a person remembers an event then he must have been in a position to have direct knowledge of the event at the time at which it happened.[46]

In what follows I shall try to show that memory is neither a necessary nor a sufficient condition for making personal identity judgements, and that in making such judgements about oneself one does not use any criterion of identity at all.

One of the immediate objections to regarding memory as a criterion of personal identity was pointed out by B.A.O. Williams. His argument is as follows:

> Suppose a man to have had previously some set of memories S, and now a different set S_1. This should presumably be the situation in which he should set about using the criterion to decide the question of his identity. But this cannot be so, for when he has memories S, and again when he has memories S_1, he is in no doubt about his identity, and so the question does not even occur to him. For it to occur to him, he would have to have S and S_1 at the same time, and so S would be included in S_1 which is contrary to the hypothesis that they are, in the relevant sense different.[47]

The second objection to regarding memory as the criterion of personal identity is pointed out by Mrinal Miri. The objection is:

> For a person can suffer a total loss of memory of all his past life (except perhaps his immediate past), without thereby ceasing either to be a person or to be identical with a person in the past. Such a person could still speak a language and communicate thoughts to other persons, retain his former habits, character and peculiarities of manner fairly intact. It would be absurd either to refuse to call him a person, or to deny his identity with the person with whom he is bodily continuous. If someone finds this doubtful, we can look at the matter from another point of view, — from the point of view of the sufferer. Suppose a brain surgeon having examined my brain, tells me that I am soon going to lose all memories of my past life, would I think that I shall, from the moment of the forecast happening, cease to exist? Certainly not. Rather I shall look forward not just to the predicted happening but to my continued life after it, with fear and perhaps hope — hope sometimes of regaining my memories, or resignation. Neither would this be fear and hope of the unknown, of 'life after death', for I know well enough what *my* continued existence after predicted happening is going to be like.[48]

These objections by themselves are enough to show that memory cannot be a criterion of personal identity. A memory theorist, however, may hold that it is not necessary that a person should actually remember all his past experiences in order to continue to be the same person. Rather, what is necessary is that a person must, under suitable circumstances, be capable of doing so, that he need not have actual memories but potential memories of his past. To counter this claim of the memory theorist we have other objections to making memory the criterion of personal identity. First, the claim that memory is the criterion of personal identity is exposed to the charge of circularity, for it is plausible to argue that remembering an experience already implies thinking of it as an experience of one's own. However, this is not a serious objection, for, as Ayer points out 'to claim an experience as one's own may consist in nothing more than a disposition to use first person language in describing it' and 'in using the first person, one need not be raising the question whether any criteria of personal identity are satisfied; otherwise, it would always be sensible to ask of any experience whether it was one's own'.[49] Even if we are able to meet the first objection in this way, the second and more serious objection still remains. The objection is this: not every experience can be remembered; otherwise each piece of remembering, which is itself one experience, would have to be remembered, and it only means that each remembering of a remembering of a remembering and so on *ad infinitum* has to be remembered. But this is absurd for it leads us to infinite regression. Thirdly, the use of memory as a criterion of personal identity involves the use of a logically prior criterion of personal identity. For, in order for us to construct the correct history, we must also know that the memories besides being coherent with each other must also be correct. And, it is only from an independent knowledge of the history of the person that we can know whether the memories are correct or not. In the case of the actual memory claims we could easily afford to overlook this objection. But the potential memory claims obviously require a prior criterion of personal identity. For when we ascribe potential memories to someone, say X, the question 'What is the criterion for thinking that the things X is claimed to have memories of should have happened to X, the very same person?' The answer to this question obviously requires another independent criterion of personal identity. Fourthly, if memory were a criterion of personal identity, then my knowledge of a past event should be based solely on my memory of that event, in the sense of being a conclusion from the remembered facts. But my judgement of remembering a

If I remember something that P, then my knowing P is not based on some evidence, or some criterion. For example, if I remember that I had a headache yesterday, then, 'I know (now) that I had a headache yesterday' is not a conclusion from the fact that I remember my having the headache yesterday. The usage of the word 'remember' is such that if any sincere statement about the past is made by employing it, then that statement is generally true. If a sincerely made statement using the expression 'remember' is made and turns out to be false, then we can conclude that the speaker does not know the meaning or the usage of the word 'remember'. As Shoemaker puts it:

> We would not be satisfied that one of our own children had learned the correct use of the word 'remember' and of the expression that indicates a past tense unless the sincere statements he made by the use of these expressions were normally true — just as we would not allow that someone knew the meaning of the word 'blue' if he typically applies it to such things as grass and trees. In this case as in many others using an expression correctly necessarily goes together with using it to make statements that are (for the most part) true ... if the language of a people were translated in a certain way and it turned out that the utterance translated as memory claims nearly always had to be regarded as false, this would surely be conclusive grounds for saying that these utterances were not memory claims at all and that the language had been mistranslated.[51]

Malcolm puts the same point by saying: 'Knowing how to use the past tense cannot be completely separated from actually using it correctly, and using it correctly cannot be completely separated from making many true statements with it'.[52] From the discussion above, it follows that if a particular statement is based on memory in the sense of being a memory statement, then there are no criteria of identity on which such statements are made. For to say that such a statement is a memory statement is to say that it is not a conclusion from anything, and therefore is not a conclusion grounded on the criteria of identity.

We shall now try to answer the question 'In which category of statements (memory statement, or memory-based statement) do the first person past tense statements such as "I broke the front window yesterday" come?' The answer to this question is crucial, for if they come under memory statements, then there are no criteria on which they are grounded. But, if they are memory-based statements, then they are conclusions that require justification in terms of the criteria of identity.

My answer to this question is that the first person past tense statements are memory statements, for, if they were memory-based statements, then (to take a typical example) the first person past tense statement 'I broke the front window yesterday' must be based on memory in the sense of being a conclusion from what I remember. It cannot be the case that I remember that I broke the window when I did not break it. What I remember must be (a) that the front window was broken, (b) that someone of a certain description broke the window, and (c) that that person was myself. It is held that (c) is a conclusion drawn from (a) and (b) in conjunction with the criterion of identity.

We said earlier that it is a necessary truth about memory that if I remember some event, then I must have been a witness to that event at the time of its occurrence. Thus, if I remember that the front window was broken yesterday, then it follows that I must have been present when the front window was broken. Accordingly, I am entitled to say 'I was present when the front window was broken.' But clearly this first person past tense statement is not based on some criterion of personal identity. It is not a conclusion drawn from some remembered fact; rather it is entailed by a certain proposition which states that I remember a past event. From this it follows that there are at best some first person past tense statements that are not based on some criterion of identity, but are memory statements. Now, if I can know without using any criterion of identity that I was present when a certain action was done, then I can also remember without using any criterion of identity that that action was done by myself if I did that action. For if I had a criterion of identity here, then I would first have to find out by applying my criterion of identity to other persons who may have been present at the time of the occurrence of the event that none of them was myself. I would first have to remember that the front window was broken, discover by applying my criterion that the person who broke the front window was not myself and then find out, by consulting my memory of breaking the window, that it was broken by me. But this is impossible.

From our discussion, therefore, it follows that first person past tense statements generally are memory statements, statements that simply report on what the speaker remembers and are not conclusions from what he remembers. Once we recognise this fact, then there cannot arise any question whether I remember the experience, or any question as to the ownership of the experience. In all such cases where one's knowledge of the past experience is based on memory, there is no room for the employment of any criteria of personal identity. No question of identity arises, and there is none to be settled by reference to the criteria of identity. For example, if I remember that I broke the front window yesterday, then the question 'Am I the person who broke the front window yesterday?' does not arise. Here a sceptic may say that it is logically possible for a person to doubt his own identity. One may be in a position in which Rip Van Winkle was when he said 'God knows! I am not myself — I'm somebody else — that is me yonder — no, that's somebody else got into my shoes. I was myself last night, but I fell asleep on the mountain, and they've changed my gun, and everything changed and I am changed and I cannot tell what's my name or who I am!'. Our reply to the sceptic will be: Our memories can be incomplete and fragmentary; and it is possible for someone to remember that a particular thing was done without having a memory of doing it. For example, we might say, 'I remember somebody putting the bookmark on page 45, but I do not recall who it was', and after some time might add 'Oh! it must be myself who put the bookmark there; for, no one else reads this book.' Here, it is not a case of drawing a conclusion from some remembered facts, but only making use of some information to make an extrapolation from some remembered facts. In other words, it is not a matter of drawing any conclusions at all, but is simply a matter of my coming to remember what I previously had not remembered.

Notes

1. B. Russell, *Analysis of Mind*, London: George Allen and Unwin, 1921, p. 18.
2. Cf. Locke, *An Essay Concerning Human Understanding*, ed. A.C. Fraser, Oxford: Oxford University Press, 1894, I, pp. 466-7 where he says: '*Person* as I take it, is the name of this self. Wherever a man finds what he calls himself, there, I think, another may say is the same person.'
3. CM, p. 180.
4. Cf. Locke's definition of a person, *Essay*, p. 446.

5. 'Meditations', II, *Philosophical Writings*, ed. E. Anscombe and Peter Geach, London, Nelson, 1959, p. 70.
6. *Essays on the Intellectual Powers of Man*, ed. A.D. Woozley, London: Macmillan, 1941, p. 203.
7. See above, pp. 68-69.
8. C.D. Broad, *The Mind and Its Place in Nature*, London: Routledge and Kegan Paul, 1925, pp. 558-62.
9. 'On the Nature of Acquaintance', *Logic and Knowledge: Essays 1901-50*, ed. by R.C. Marsh, London: Routledge and Kegan Paul, 1956, p. 162.
10. Cf. 'Meditations', II.
11. *Essays on the Intellectual Powers of Man*, p. 203.
12. Cf. CM, pp. 153-4.
13. *A Treatise of Human Nature*, pp. 251-2.
14. Ibid., p. 252.
15. Ibid., p. 253.
16. pp. 17-18.
17. Hume says in a well-known passage: 'For my part, when I enter most intimately into what I call *myself*, I always stumble on some particular perception or other, of heat or cold, light or shade, love or hatred, pain or pleasure. I never can catch *myself* at any time without a perception and never can observe anything but the perception'. (*A Treatise on Human Nature*, p. 252.) And 'When I turn my reflection on *myself*, I never can perceive the *self* without some one or more perception; nor can I perceive anything but the perception. It is the composition of these, therefore, which forms the self'. (*A Treatise on Human Nature*, p. 634).
18. *A Treatise on Human Nature*, p. 67.
19. Cf. CM, p. 157.
20. CM, p. 158.
21. CM, p. 50.
22. CM, p. 160.
23. CM, |p. 161.
24. CM, pp. 160-1.
25. P.F. Strawson, 'Persons', *Minnesota Studies in the Philosophy of Science*, vol. II, ed. H. Feigl, M. Seriven and G. Maxwell, University of Minnesota Press, 1958.
26. Cf. CM 50.
27. S. Shoemaker, *Self-Knowledge and Self-Identity*, New York: Cornell University Press, 1967, p. 223.
28. Cf. *Self-Knowledge and Self-Identity*, p. 224.
29. On pp. 53-56 of Chapter II, I have shown the absurd consequences of holding the view that 'pain' is the name of a sensation.
30. Cf. PI 381.
31. Cf. CM, p. 171.
32. CM, p. 188.
33. Cf. CM, p. 189.
34. 'On the Nature of Acquaintance', p. 131.
35. 'Hume on Personal Identity', *Philosophical Review*, vol. 64 (1955), pp. 571-89.
36. *Individuals*, London: Methuen, 1959, p. 37.
37. *An Essay Concerning Human Understanding*, I, p. 458.
38. 'Personal Identity', *Mind*, vol. 50 (1941), p. 340.
39. 'On the Nature of Acquaintance', *Logic and Knowledge: Essays 1901-1956*, ed. R.C. Marsh, p. 138.
40. *The Philosophy of Logical Atomism*, ed. D. Pears; London: Collins, 1972, p. 277.

41. *A Treatise on Human Nature*, p. 261.
42. *Foundations of Empirical Knowledge*, London: Macmillan, 1953, p. 142.
43. *Identity and Spatio-Temporal Continuity*, Oxford: Oxford University Press, 1967, p. 43.
44. 'On Knowing Who One Is', *Common Factor* (No. 4, 1966), p. 52.
45. 'On Knowing Who One Is', p. 53.
46. A little later in this chapter, I try to show that this necessary truth or rather the fact that it is a necessary truth about memory leads not to the conclusion that memory is a criterion of personal identity but to a very different conclusion, namely, that in asserting the first person past tense statements one does not use any criterion of personal identity at all.
47. B.A.O. Williams, 'Personal Identity and Individuation', *Proceedings of the Aristotelian Society*, LVII (1956-7), pp. 229-52.
48. Mrinal Miri, 'Memory and Personal Identity', *Mind*, vol. LXXXII, no. 325, January 1973, p. 3.
49. A.J. Ayer, *The Problem of Knowledge,*, Harmondsworth: Penguin Books, 1974, p. 196.
50. Cf. S. Shoemaker, *Self-Knowledge and Self-Identity*, pp. 133-4, 229.
51. 'Memory', *Encyclopedia of Philosophy*, ed. Paul Edwards, Macmillan and Free Press, 1967.
52. 'Three Lectures on Memory', *Knowledge and Certainty*, Englewood Cliffs, NJ: Prentice Hall, Inc., 1963, p. 196.

4 KNOWLEDGE OF OTHER PERSONS

Our argument in the last chapter led to the conclusion that there is no special epistemic problem of self-knowledge and personal identity. I propose in this chapter to show that there is no epistemic problem about the knowledge of other minds and their identity either. For it is a basic feature of our life that we know that the other walking and talking figures having human shape and form, that we hear and see, have minds. To support this thesis I do two things. One: I discuss the basic assumptions that give rise to the problem of other minds, and also I examine the various arguments offered by the theorists to account for our knowledge of the other minds. Two: I argue for the thesis that third person personal identity judgements are based on the similarity of bodily appearance and other behavioural facts (including the verbal behaviour) of other persons at various times. To support this thesis I have critically examined and rejected various objections to regarding bodily identity as a criterion for asserting third person identity judgements. In the main I have discussed the change-of-body argument as put forward by Shoemaker.

We said in the previous chapter that self-knowledge is possible through the knowledge of others. In this chapter, we shall try to show how we come to have knowledge of other selves. The question 'How do I know other selves?' I take as equivalent to the question 'How do I know that the walking and talking figures which I see and hear have sensations, feelings, and thoughts, or in short have minds?' The last question can be replaced by 'How do I know other minds?' The reason why other minds present a problem in traditional theories is the belief of these philosophers in one or all of the following natural assumptions:

> (i) All our 'simple' experiences are always 'named' by a kind of ostensive procedure that is essentially private. The words which express our simple experiences have meaning only in the sense that they 'stand for' or label certain kinds of experience which are utterly distinct from any publicly observable

behaviour or physical changes that might regularly accompany them.

(ii) One's having a sensation is a necessary and sufficient condition for knowing that sensation. In other words, it is claimed that if I am in pain, then *ipso facto* I know that I am in pain. It is held on this view that the having of a sensation entails an immediate knowledge of its character and identity.

(iii) I have direct knowledge of my experiences.

(iv) One can never be directly aware of another's sensations. By this they mean that one can never be aware that another is in pain in the way in which one is aware of one's own pain, and that the degree of certainty involved in the two cases is different.

The traditional problem of other minds, 'How is one to discover that there are experiences other than one's own, such as observations, feelings, sensations, and that such experiences belong to some other minds?', arises from the assumptions (i) to (iv) as follows: To solve the problem of other minds is to discover the criteria, or the tests, and verification that could ever be possible for anyone to carry out to know that heterobiographical statements, for example, 'He is giddy', 'You are thinking', 'You are in pain', and the like asserted by him are true. This discovery obviously can be made either directly or indirectly. By 'direct discovery' we mean that it will be made either by sensory perception or by some other sort of intuition. And by 'indirect discovery' we mean that it will be made by inference. Clearly by virtue of the assumptions (iii) and (iv) it follows that I cannot directly know that other people have thoughts, sensations, and feelings, nor can we directly know other minds by some extra sensory perception, namely, intuition, where 'knowing directly' implies that no question arises of how they are known and no question arises of any evidence being required to support that knowledge. As it stands, the view that we can have direct knowledge of others' sensations, thoughts and feelings, would be false. For by assumption (iii) only the subject can know without evidence that he has a sensation. Therefore, such knowledge is *ex hypothesi* ruled out to anyone other than the subject. It is for this reason that even the most strenuous intuitionists do not include this discovery among the things that I know by direct intuition. So it is held that one can know by inference only that others have minds, that they have feelings, thoughts and sensations. I can know that others have minds by infering from the behaviour and other related facts which these bodies exhibit, and to which I have access. The problem now is 'How is such inference to be carried out?', and, in particular, 'How could such an inference ever be justified?'

Descartes, thinking about the existence of other finite, created, thinking and unextended substances, in short, other human minds, uses the form of an argument from analogy. In arguing from analogy for the existence of other minds, Descartes is not alone. He is accompanied by practically all empiricist philosophers. While Berkeley argues for the existence of other minds from analogy, Locke simply 'presume[s] it will be easily granted me, that there are such ideas in man's mind. Every one is conscious of them in himself; and men's words and actions will satisfy him that they are in others'.[1] Recent empiricist philosophers like Ayer also support the argument from analogy by saying 'that many of the statements which one makes about the experiences of others are fully justifiable on the basis of one's own'.[2] To argue from analogy is to argue on the principle that if a property A has been found to be generally associated with something B, then any property similar to A is very likely to be associated with a thing very similar to B. In our day-to-day life, we make use of the argument from analogy as an alternative to direct observation. For example, if a doctor finds that the symptoms of two diseases are in some respects similar and he has been able to find out that one of them is caused by a particular type of bacterium, then he may infer by analogy that the other disease is also caused by the same bacterium and try to detect it. In the case of other minds the argument from analogy was clearly stated by J.S. Mill. He says:

> other human beings have feelings like me, because, first, they have bodies like me, which I know, in my own case, to be the antecedent condition of feelings; and because, secondly, they exhibit the acts and other outward signs, which in my own case I know by experience to be caused by feelings. I am conscious in myself of a series of facts connected by a uniform sequence, of which the beginning is modifications of my body, the middle is feelings, the end is outward demeanour. In the case of other human beings I have the evidence of my senses for the first and last links of the series, but not for the intermediate link. I find, however, that the sequence between the first and last is as

regular and constant in those other cases as it is in mine. In my own case I know that the first link produces the last through the intermediate link, and could not produce it without. Experience, therefore, obliges me to conclude that there must be an intermediate link, which must either be the same in others as in myself, or a different one: I must either believe them to be alive, or to be *automatons*: and by believing them to be alive, that is, by supposing the link to be of the same nature as in the case of which I have experience, and which is in all other respects similar, I bring other human beings, as phenomena, under the same generalizations which I know by experience to be the true theory of my own existence.[3]

To justify this argument from analogy he adds:

And in doing so I conform to the legitimate rules of experimental enquiry. The process is exactly parallel to that by which Newton proved that the force which keeps the planets in their orbits is identical with that by which an apple falls to the ground. It was not incumbent on Newton to prove the impossibility of its being any other force; he was thought to have made out his point when he had simply shown that no other force need be supposed. We know the existence of other beings by generalization from the knowledge of our own: the generalization merely postulates that what experience shows to be a mark of the existence of something within the sphere of our consciousness, may be concluded to be a mark of the same things beyond the sphere.[4]

On the face of it, the argument from analogy for the existence of other minds seems quite persuasive, but on a critical examination all its persuasive powers vanish and the following drawbacks become quite clear.
(a) This objection applies not only to the argument from analogy for the existence of other minds but to the argument from analogy in general. Any argument from analogy is non-deductive. No matter how certain one may be of one's premises, there is always the possibility of error in the conclusion. In most cases, this uncertainty can be overcome by finding out direct evidence for the truth of the conclusion. In the case of the other minds this alterna-

tive is impossible. The trouble in the case of the inference (analogy) to other minds is that it is incurably indirect, for one can never be directly aware of the mind of another person. There is no way of making sure exactly what is going on in the mind of the other person. This argument, thus, does not give us sufficient or adequate reasons to believe in the existence of other minds.

(b) The analogical argument provides very weak inductive reasoning, for its conclusions are drawn from one case only, namely, that of the person who makes use of the argument from analogy for the existence of other minds. Therefore, it does not establish its conclusion with any adequate degree of certainty. The analogical argument for the existence of other minds could be more certain if it had been drawn from a number of cases. Moreover, the characteristics and behaviour of one person markedly differ from the characteristics and behaviour of another. On this theory, we would never be able to know that others also have the same feelings as I have, when I show certain characteristic signs or behave in a particular fashion. Thus, if I generalise from one case only, namely, my own, then it could only be called an irresponsible generalisation. As Wittgenstein puts it 'How can I generalize the *one* case so irresponsibly?' (*PI* 293).

(c) The argument from analogy for the existence of other minds is incoherent, for the philosophers who support it start with the assumption that the other walking and talking figures may have pains, feelings and thoughts. Having made the assumption, they try to justify it (their belief) by arguing from analogy. But this is a mistake; because, on the sceptic's theory the statements like 'He is in pain', or 'He is thinking' do not make sense, and therefore carry no meaning for him. If he had a criterion for understanding these statements, then he would straightaway apply that criterion, and thus, would not need an argument from analogy.

Here, it may be objected that it is quite easy for the sceptic to understand the statement 'He is in pain.' For he understands the statement 'I am in pain' fully well, the statement 'He is in pain' means that he has the same thing which I have when I have a pain.[5] But, this is a fruitless endeavour. It requires this sceptic to know the criterion (and he has none) for establishing that he has the same pain as someone else has when he (the other person) has pain. To repeat a point already made: if he could give this criterion he would be left with no use for the argument from analogy, and if he could not give such a criterion then also the argument from analogy would be useless for him.

(d) The argument from analogy for the existence of other minds (as stated above) assumes the following:

(i) That a person can empirically discover the required psycho-physical relationship in his own case; and

(ii) that having discovered such co-relations between the psychic and the physical to hold in one's own case, one is entitled to assume that they hold in the case of the other persons as well.

We have shown earlier that assumption (ii) is a weak inductive inference.[6] But this does not lead to the demolition of the argument from analogy. All it does is to prove that this knowledge of other minds is not certain but only probable. Assumption (i), however, is the crux of the argument, or if we are able to show that (i) is false then the argument would not even get started; and consequently we shall not be required even to refute (ii) in order to refute the argument from analogy.

The first assumption supposes that my knowledge of the psycho-physical relationships in my own case is purely empirical. But this is false, for, if my knowledge of the psycho-physical relations in my own case were entirely empirical, then how could I ever begin discovering these relationships? — that is, how did I ever discover the first one? — or to put the question differently, how did I obtain the knowledge of my bodily states that I would need to have in order to discover my co-relations between bodily states and psychological states? Obviously, I cannot have known my bodily states from visual, auditory, gustatory, olfactory, or kinaesthetic sensations, for, in order to do this I would already have to have knowledge of a psychological relationship; I would have to know that the occurrence of certain sensations indicates, and therefore is correlated with, the existence of certain bodily states. Nor do I make this discovery by observing my body, that it was in a certain state. This can be illustrated by the fact that in our day-to-day life we do not conclude from the observation of some of our own bodily states that we are angry or sad.

There is no other method available to a person for making this empirical discovery of the connection of his mental states with his bodily states. However, it may be said here that we can have knowledge of our own bodies which is not based on observation, nor is inferred from sensations. We seem to have such knowledge, for instance, of our own voluntary bodily movements. But if it is the case that sometimes I just know that my body is in a certain state, then in these cases there exists a psycho-physical relationship between my having beliefs of a certain kind and the facts about my body. That is, between my having such beliefs and their being true. The question 'Are the relationships between psychological and physical features of a person contingent?' naturally arises now. The answer to this question is crucial for, if these relationships are contingent then it is conceivable that they might have not been held, that is, that such beliefs generally could be false. But if such beliefs generally could be false, then either I have empirical grounds for thinking that my beliefs of this sort are in fact generally true, in which case they are not evidenceless after all; or, I do not have such empirical grounds, in which case my beliefs may, for all I know, be generally false, and therefore do not constitute knowledge even if they happen to be true. Therefore, it is clear that if psycho-physical relationships were contingent, there could be no way in which one could discover, even in one's own case, that such relationships hold.

(e) The validity of the argument from analogy for the existence of other minds implies that one must learn from one's own case alone what it means to have a mental attribute, say pain. But this is absurd. If 'pain' is given a meaning entirely by an ostensive procedure in which I am the only participant, so that it refers to a domain of 'objects' of which only I am (or can be) aware, then there is really no sense to the idea that the others can have pains too. Indeed, such a procedure makes no distinction between my pain and pain *simpliciter*. On this view, the two expressions would have precisely the same meaning. But this is wrong. To have a concept of an experience is not to have the concept of one's own experience alone. Rather, it is to have a notion of another's experience and to have some method of distinguishing my experiences from the experiences of the other persons. Otherwise, the distinctions between 'my experience', 'his experience' and 'your experience' would make no sense at all. As Strawson puts it:

> It is a necessary condition of one's ascribing states of consciousness, experiences to oneself, in the way one does, that one should also ascribe them or be prepared to ascribe them, to others who are not oneself ... The main point here is a purely logical one: the idea of a predicate is correlative with that of a

range of distinguishable individuals of which the predicate can be significantly, though not necessarily truly, affirmed.[7]

Moreover, we have already said that if each one of us had to name a sensation, say, pain, from his own case, then no public use of the word 'pain' would be possible.[8] For we would never be able to know what the other person means by 'pain'.

(f) Lastly, the validity of the argument from analogy for the existence of other minds implies the possibility of a private language. We have already shown that a private language is impossible.[9] Moreover, in the argument from analogy for the existence of other minds we tend to assume a little man (the self, the ego, the knowing subject, or one's own mind) who sits inside the skull and looks out through the eyes — 'the windows of the soul'. We have already in the chapter on self-knowledge and personal identity shown that such a view of the mind is absurd.

The foregoing discussion has proved that the argument from analogy for the existence of other minds is invalid and its conclusion is false. We shall now consider another argument offered by H.H. Price for the existence of other minds.[10] He says: 'One's evidence for the existence of other minds is derived primarily from the understanding of language'.[11] Here Price uses the word 'language' in a wide sense which includes not only speech and writing, but signals and gestures such as believing and pointing also. In other words, we may say that the evidence for the existence of other minds, for Price, comes from communication situations. His argument runs as follows: If a foreign body (by a foreign body, he means a body other than mine; it can even be a body which does not have human form) utters noises which one understands like 'Look! There is a body' and if these noises give one some new information, then, 'this simple occurrence of hearing an utterance, understanding it, and then verifying it for oneself provides some evidence that the foreign body which uttered the noise is animated by a mind like my own'.[12] He goes so far as to hold that these informative sounds need not be produced by a human body. He says: 'If the rustling of the leaves of an oak tree formed intelligible words conveying new information to me, and if gorse-bushes made intelligent gestures, I should have evidence that the oak or the gorse-bush was animated by an intelligence like my own'.[13]

Though this argument differs sharply from the classical analogical argument, yet the reasoning presented by Price is still analogical in form. He holds that I know in my own case, by introspection, that when a certain combination of sounds are uttered by me they are 'symbols of acts of spontaneous thinking'; therefore, similar combinations of sounds, not produced by me, probably function as instruments to an act of spontaneous thinking, which in this case is not my own'.[14]

The main objection against Price's argument is that no amount of intelligible sounds coming from an oak tree or a gorse-bush could create any probability that it has a mind. For it is the characteristic of a being having a mind that it understands the words produced or listened to by it. By 'understanding' we mean that it can make correct application of the words in question. The correct application of a word involves looking, pointing, fetching, carrying, reaching for, and going to the right things and not to the wrong ones. Whereas a child or a human being can do such activities, a tree cannot. Therefore, the fact that an object was a source of intelligible sounds, or any other signs, would not be enough by itself to establish that it had thoughts or sensations, or in other words, a mind. How the intelligible sounds, if any, are produced by an oak tree can be a scientific problem; but the explanation could never be that the tree has a mind. All of us believe that it is not merely the case that things which do not have the human form, or anything like it do not satisfy the criterion for thinking, but we also believe that they cannot satisfy the criterion for thinking. This is what Wittgenstein had in mind when he said: 'We only say of a human being and what is like one that it thinks' (*PI* 360).

Recent empiricist philosophers attempt another solution to the problem of other minds. A.J. Ayer says 'I must define material things and my own self in terms of their empirical manifestations — that is, in terms of the behaviour of bodies, and ultimately in terms of sense contents'.[15] From this, it follows that he defines the existence of other selves in terms of the actual and hypothetical occurrences. But this is wrong, for, while it is significant to analyse material objects in terms of empirical manifestations, we cannot talk about other selves on the same lines, because this amounts to restricting our considerations to their outward behaviour only. We may exhaust the description of material objects, but the description of persons cannot be so exhausted.[16] As Karl Popper puts it:

> It is the particular, the unique and concrete individual, which

cannot be approached by rational methods, and not the abstract universal. Science can describe general types of landscape, for example, or of man, but it can never exhaust one single individual landscape or one single individual man ... the unique individual and his unique actions and experiences and relations to others can never be fully rationalised.[17]

Having proved that the classical argument for analogy as well as some modified versions of it are unable to help us solve the problem of other minds, I shall now try to show that the assumptions of which the problem of other minds is the result are erroneous, though natural; and that when these errors are exposed the problem is dissolved. We have already shown the absurd consequences of the view that 'pain', or for that matter all our mental concepts, are the names of certain kinds of sensation[18] (called 'simple experiences' in the first assumption). The second assumption is erroneous, for having a sensation is neither a necessary nor a sufficient condition for describing it, for the following reasons: First, knowing a sensation involves the knowledge of the language. In absence of the knowledge of the language one would be unable to describe what sensations one is having. Therefore, even if one regards the having of a sensation a necessary condition for knowing it, this itself is not sufficient. Secondly, if knowing a sensation were having the sensation, then it would be analytically impossible for anyone to have knowledge of the sensations and feelings of others. In such a situation no argument would help us in proving or knowing the other minds. In the chapter on self-knowledge and personal identity we have already shown that one does not have privileged access to one's own mind. Our reason for denying the privileged access to a state of one's own mind put briefly is: Just because there is no such thing as my knowing from evidence that I am in pain, there can be no such thing as my being in a special position to know without evidence that I am in pain. So, assumption (iii) is also false. Now we shall deal with assumption (iv). Assumption (iv) can be divided into two parts:

(a) One person can never know that another person is in pain in the same way in which he knows that he is. In other words, one cannot know directly that the other person is in pain.

(b) One can never be as certain of the other's pain as one is of one's own.

(iva) is a consequence of the theories of mind that I have discussed in the chapter on self-knowledge and personal identity. On these theories it is not only the case that one cannot have direct knowledge of other minds, but also that it is logically impossible for one to have such knowledge at all. The fact that these theories try to make persons knowable to themselves and unknowable to persons other than themselves is itself sufficient proof that these theories are mistaken.[19]

However, Ryle and Wittgenstein differ with regard to the method in which one comes to know about other minds. Ryle maintains that I know about others in much the same way as I know about myself, that is, inductively. He says: 'The sorts of things that I can find out about myself are the same as the sorts of things that I can find out about other people, and the methods of finding out are much the same'.[20] The method of coming to know about other minds is by observing the behaviour of others. 'Our knowledge of other people and of ourselves depends upon noticing how they and we behave.[21] The term behaviour includes not only bodily behaviour, but linguistic behaviour also. As Ryle puts it: 'there is one tract of human behaviour on which we pre-eminently rely. When the person examined has learned to talk in a language well known to us, we use part of his talk as the primary source of our information about him, that part namely which is spontaneous, frank and unprepared'.[22]

Wittgenstein, on the other hand, maintains, that the first person psychological statements are not knowledge-claims. Therefore, he concludes, one needs no method of knowing one's own mental states.[23] The third person psychological statements (that is, the assertions that show that others have minds) are knowledge-claims. They require justification. And therefore the question 'How do you know ...?' can be raised about them. Wittgenstein's view seems to me to be correct. For, in our day-to-day life, we all make psychological assertions about ourselves and we do not use any method, including observation of behaviour, in asserting them. But in the case of the third person psychological assertions we do have to observe certain facts (which we shall discuss in what follows) to assert them. These facts reflect the mental states directly.[24] So (iva) which says that one cannot know other minds directly is false. We have already shown that one can know others' pain with the same certainty with which one knows about one's own pain.[25] It follows that (ivb) also is false.

With this we are able to show that the assumptions which gave birth to the problem of other minds are all false. Therefore, the problem of other minds is not a genuine problem; it is a pseudo problem.

For Wittgenstein the question 'How do we know other minds?' is reduced to the concrete particular question 'How do we know that the others are in pain?' We have shown in the chapter on privacy and private language that the fact that we attribute pains to others is a composite part of the total behaviour that belongs to our form of life. We do not attribute pains to stones, tables and chairs, because our attitude towards a stone and towards a being having human body and shape is different. As Wittgenstein puts it: 'My attitude towards him is an attitude towards a soul. I am not of the opinion that he has a soul', and 'The human body is the best picture of the human soul' (*PI*, Part II, p. 178). The answer to the question 'How do I know that others have pains?' can only be that I know it from the way they behave and from their assertions that they are in pain. And the question 'Why do we regard this as grounds for ascribing pains to others?' can only be answered by saying, 'It is because we have been trained in this way'. This can be illustrated by taking the example of a chicken-sexer or a tea-taste expert. When asked 'Why does he regard the two-day-old chick to be a cock when it grows up?' or 'Why does he regard the particular tea to be put in grade A?' he is apt to reply (and that is the correct reply too) by saying, 'I have received the proper training.' This question concerns a technique and the 'questions of technique cannot be answered by any number of questions of causal conditioning: they are questions of quite different types'.[26] So, by virtue of the training we have received we know that the other walking and talking figures which have bodies similar to mine, have minds. And, if anyone makes the classical challenge 'I can never really know whether the others have minds', we are entitled to sympathise with him and say: 'Then do something about it!'

The question 'How do I know the other minds or selves?' besides asking for the criterion of individuation also asks for the criterion of identification, in other words, it asks for the criterion by which we can know that 'X at 2 is the same as X at 52'. To account for identity, in the history of philosophy, two types of theories, one: the psychological type, and two: the physical type (which have been thought to be rivals of each other), have been put forward. We have already considered one of them, namely, the memory theory of personal identity.[27] For the same reasons for which memory cannot be the criterion of personal identity in the first person statements, it can also not be the criterion of personal identity in the third person statement. Throughout our discussion of the memory theory of personal identity, the other rival theory, that a person is a physical body of some sort, and that personal identity consists in the bodily identity, has loomed in the background.

In day-to-day life, our identity judgements about other persons are generally based on similarity of bodily appearance. However, there are philosophers who think that bodily identity cannot be regarded as the criterion of personal identity at all. Their objections to the view that similarity of appearance can be regarded as the criterion of personal identity are as follows:

(a) Two different persons can look exactly alike (as in the case of twins).

(b) The appearance of one and the same person at different times may be totally different (for instance, the infant becomes a teenager, the teenager a youth, the youth a middle-aged person and so on).

(c) The two objections (a) and (b) mentioned above are not as serious as this objection. We shall call it the change-of-body argument. It states that it is logically possible for a person to change his body with some other person. Locke was the first philosopher to raise this objection. He remarks 'should the soul of a prince, carrying with it the consciousness of the prince's past life enter and inform the body of a cobbler, as soon as deserted of his own soul, every one sees that he would be the same person with the prince accountable only for the prince's action'.[28]

Shoemaker puts the same objection in a more forceful manner. He tells the story of two men, Brown and Robinson, who undergo brain operations.[29] Their brains are removed from their bodies. At the end of the operation, by some mistake, Brown's brain is fitted into Robinson's head and Robinson's brain into Brown's. The man with Brown's body and Robinson's brain dies immediately, the other with Brown's brain and Robinson's body regains consciousness. The resulting person has apparently the memories of Brown and the body of Robinson and 'over a period of time he is observed to display all the personality traits, mannerisms, interests, likes and dislikes, and so on that had previously characterised Brown, and to act and talk in ways completely alien to the old Robinson'.[30] Shoemaker calls this resulting person Brownson. The question naturally arises now, 'Should we regard the resulting person Brownson to be really Brown or Robinson?' Shoemaker does not commit himself to any positive answer to it in his book. But, in his article 'On Knowing Who One is' he says:

> If, as I believe, it would be reasonable in this case to say that Brownson (i.e., the surviving person), remembers events in Brown's life, it would also be reasonable to conclude that Brownson is Brown. These conclusions would be most compelling if virtually all of Brownson's memories correspond to events in Brown's past history. In any event this seems to be a case in which the question of whether X is the same person as Y ultimately turns, not as whether X is bodily continuous with Y but as whether X can remember events in Y's life'.[31]

We shall now consider these objections one by one. The assertion in objection (a), namely, that two different persons may look exactly alike, is true. But, to say that two different persons are exactly alike is not to say that they are identical. The only case in which the identity and the exact similarity can be distinguished is that of the body — the same body and the exactly similar body do make a difference. Thus, to omit bodily criterion of personal identity is to take away the content from the idea of personal identity.

Objection (b) expresses a truism. It is a fact that there is a change in the appearance of a person in the course of his life. This objection becomes more forceful when it is supported by the biologist's discovery that the cells in the human body are completely changed over a period of six years. To this objection, we may reply that though it is correct to say that the appearance of a person changes over a period of time, these changes are very gradual and that the new appearance resembles the old appearance in too general a way to be described. It is just because of these resemblances that we are able to recognise a person when we meet him after a considerable lapse of time.

The third objection (c) looks quite forceful at first sight. Its forcefulness, however, disappears when we realise that some character traits and mannerism are more suited to one body than to the other. For example, in the prince-cobbler body interchange case the prince's body might include the sort of face that just could not express the cobbler's morose suspiciousness, the cobbler's is a face no expression of which could be taken for the fastidious arrogance of the prince. These 'coulds' are not just factual but logical. Such expressions on these features might be unthinkable. As B.A.O. Williams says: 'the concept of bodily interchange cannot be taken for granted, and that there are even logical limits to what we should be prepared to say in this direction. What these limits are, cannot be foreseen — one has to consider the cases and for this one has to see the cases. The converse is also true, that it is difficult to tell in advance how far certain features may suddenly seem to express something quite unexpected. But there are limits, and when this is recognised, the idea of interchange of personalities seems very odd.'[32]

From the above discussion, it follows that bodily identity can be regarded as a criterion of personal identity. This thesis is supported by the fact that in our day-to-day life we pass judgements of identity on other persons on the basis of similarity of bodily appearance and other behavioural criteria.

Just as it is a 'form of life' for us to know other minds, similarly it is a form of our life to know about the continuity of the other minds. We grow into the mastery of this system. To say that we are taught this art of knowing other minds and their identity is misleading, though it may be said that we learn it. The technique of knowing the identity of the other minds includes many observational facts about others, but the primary among them is the bodily appearance.

Notes

1. *Essay Concerning Human Understanding*, Introduction.
2. 'One's Knowledge of Other Minds', *Philosophical Essays*, London: Macmillan, 1954, pp. 191-214.
3. *An Examination of Sir William Hamilton's Philosophy*, London: Longmans, Green and Co., 2nd edn, 1865, pp. 208-9.

4. Ibid., p. 209.
5. 'it is no explanation to say: the supposition that he has a pain is simply the supposition that he has the same as I. For *that* part of the grammar is quite clear to me: that is that one will say that the stove has the same experience as I, if one says: it is in pain and I am in pain' (PI 350).
6. See above, p. 99.
7. *Individuals*, London: Methuen, 1959, p. 99.
8. See above, pp. 56-57.
9. See above, Chapter Two.
10. 'Our Evidence for the Existence of Other Minds', *Philosophy* XIII (1938), pp. 424-56.
11. Ibid., p. 429.
12. Ibid., p. 430.
13. Ibid., p. 436.
14. Ibid., p. 446.
15. *Language, Truth and Logic*, London: Gollancz, 1967, p. 130.
16. Cf. Margaret Chatterjee, *Our Knowledge of Other Selves*, Delhi: Asia Publishing House, 1963, Chapter III.
17. *The Open Society and its Enemies*, vol. II, London: Routledge and Keagan Paul, 1950.
18. Chapter Two, pp. 52-57.
19. Cf. S. Shoemaker, *Self-Knowledge and Self-Identity*, p. 166.
20. CM, p. 149.
21. CM, p. 173.
22. CM, p. 173.
23. We have already discussed this in detail in Chapter Two.
24. For a detailed discussion, see above second chapter.
25. In the second chapter.
26. G. Ryle, 'Sensations'.
27. See above, Chapter Three.
28. *Essay Concerning Human Understanding*, I, p. 457.
29. *Self-Knowledge and Self-Identity*, pp. 23-4.
30. *Self-Knowledge and Self-Identity*, p. 24.
31. *Common Factor*, p. 55.
32. 'Personal Identity and Individuation'.

CONCLUDING NOTE

In this study, we have shown that there is no epistemological problem about minds, mine or others'. Those philosophers who thought that minds present epistemological problems were either bewitched of their intelligence by means of language, or they attempted to ask and answer questions in the way the natural scientists do. We have shown that these problems about minds disappear when we put relevant facts about them before us undistorted.

In the first chapter I showed that we need not posit any private entities such as sense-data out of which the mind is said to construct things or through the mediacy of which all its perceptions occur in order to account for observation. The fact, on the contrary, is that we are directly presented with the objects outside us. This fact was exploited by us in the second chapter where we said that no private language is needed to record our experiences; for all our mental experiences are public with no private components. In this chapter, we also showed that private language is impossible, and that the term 'private language' embodies a category mistake. In the third chapter we utilised the conclusions of the first two chapters — namely, sensations are neither private, nor do we need a private language to express them — to show that we do not know ourselves and about our identity by means of any theory or private method like introspection and intuition to which we have a privileged access, but that our knowledge of ourselves and of our identity is a fundamental feature of our life. Finally, in the fourth chapter, I have shown that there is no special problem of our knowledge of other minds, and the identity of other persons. In our view it is a basic feature of our life that we know that other walking and talking figures, having human form and shape, which we see and hear, have minds. The identity of other persons, also does not present any problem to us. For, as we have shown, we know about the identity of other persons from their bodily appearance and other behavioural facts.

In our opinion, therefore, the mind of a person is not something mysterious, to be known by some theory or private method, but it is revealed to us in linguistic and non-linguistic behaviour as occurring in the complex of conditions in which that person is situated. The term 'behaviour' is used here to refer not merely to the present, short-term behaviour but to future and past behaviour as well. It is natural for us to distinguish between an automaton and a person, between a living being and a corpse. We ascribe mind only to a living being and not to an automaton, however perfect it may be, or to a corpse. 'Why do we do so?' and 'How do we do so?' are on our view, spurious questions. They are spurious, because to do so is a basic feature of our life; and no genuine question can be asked and no answer can be given to a question about a basic feature of life. This is demonstrated by the fact that we do not ask questions like 'Why do we stand on our legs?' or 'How do we stand on our legs?'

Our thesis that the mind is not a mysterious something is amply supported by the fact that the science of psychology is based on the presupposition that we do have knowledge of minds. What we have shown further is that we gain this knowledge through a large complex of intersubjectively identifiable factors such as linguistic and non-linguistic behaviour, actions and intentions, of persons. The present study is not committed to any specific methodology, as it is done at the level of ordinary language analysis: it remains neutral to the method to be adopted by the psychologist in investigating mental phenomena. It is open to him to organise and systematise knowledge of minds by means of any of the available methods; for instance by observing the bodily behaviour of the persons concerned, or by analysing the verbal reactions to a given set of stimuli, or by any other method in tune with the demands of his investigation.

INDEX

analogy 2, 47, 78, 97, 98, 99
analytic statement 51
Anscombe, G.E.M. 66n
argument
  analogical 102
  from analogy 2, 98, 99, 100, 101, 102, 104
  from causation 20, 28
  from differential certainty 19, 24, 25
  from illusion 19, 20, 24
  from hallucination 19, 20, 24
  from physiology of perception 20, 28
  from short causal chain 31
  from time-lag 31
  from verification 19, 24, 25
Armstrong, D.M. 33n
associationist theory 73
atom 36
Augustine, St. 1, 70
Austin, J.L. 33n
Ayer, A.J. 19, 20, 50, 84, 87, 94n, 97, 103

behaviour 3, 7, 33, 42, 45, 51, 60, 66n, 68, 96, 99, 103, 105, 111, 112
  bodily 79, 80, 105, 112
  linguistic 7, 105
  pain 47, 58
behaviourism 3, 4
  analytic 2, 3
  logical 2, 3
  metaphysical 2
  methodological 2
behaviourist 3, 4
  logical 4, 7
Berkeley 1, 13, 14, 16, 97
bodily
  criterion of personal identity 68, 108
  identity 89, 95, 107
  states 100
body 46, 47, 48, 69, 75, 77, 78, 83, 84, 97, 100, 101, 102, 106, 108, 109

brain 28, 107, 108
  process 7
Broad, C.D. 70, 93n
bundle theory 73, 75

Carnap, R. 37
cartesian 4, 5, 70
category mistake 6, 34, 50, 66, 66n3, 110
casual question 29, 30
cause of pain 14
certainty 40, 41, 42, 43, 44, 45, 46, 96, 99, 106
  mathematical 45
  psychological 45
change-of-body argument 95, 107
Chatterjee, M. 110n
code 34
communicate 56, 86
communication 11, 102
concept
  formation 52
  of acquisition 52, 60
  of a person 77
  of retention 52, 61, 65
  sensation specifying 60
conscious 71, 72, 79, 97
consciousness 53, 54, 60, 72, 74, 84, 98, 101, 108
corrigible statements 26
criteria 3, 4, 5, 46, 68, 72, 79, 82, 84, 89, 90
  behavioural 2, 4, 7, 109
criterion 4, 7, 44, 46, 47, 49, 55, 62, 63, 65, 68, 78, 79, 83, 84, 85, 86, 88, 95, 99, 103
  of identification 106
  of identity 46, 49, 50, 80, 85, 88, 90, 91, 92
  of individuating 82
  of personal identity 85, 86, 87, 91, 92, 94, 107, 109
  of possession 46

definition 65
  ostensive 38, 52, 58, 60, 61, 66n
  stipulative 52

Index

Descartes, R. 1, 4, 70, 97
discovery 13
   direct 96
   indirect 96
dream 20, 22
dreaming 71
dualism 2

elements of inference 16
Entity 70, 71, 83
   non-physical 83
   private 5
   substantival 7
experience 5, 38, 81, 87, 88, 91, 95, 97, 98, 101, 110

feel 43, 44, 46, 55
first person
   identity 6
   identity judgement 88
   language 87
   psychological statements 69, 70, 78, 79, 80, 89, 105
   statement 69, 107
form of life 6, 58, 65, 66, 68, 106, 109

grammar 54, 56, 57, 110

habits 62, 63, 86
   speech 62
hallucination 24, 25
Hume, David 1, 19, 72, 73, 82, 84, 93

'I' 68, 69, 70, 73, 81
'I know' 40, 41, 42, 44
ideas 1, 2, 14, 19, 72
identity 50, 54, 82, 83, 84, 85, 86, 88, 92, 107, 109, 111
   judgement 83, 84, 88
   of other person 6
   statements 82
illusion 21, 22, 23, 24, 60
images 50
impressions 9, 19, 32, 72
'in' 17
incorrigible statements 26, 27
index word 81
inference 96, 97, 99
   elements of 16
   inductive 100
infinite regress 72

introspection 2, 6, 68, 74, 75, 103, 111
intuition 96, 111
invention 13

Jones, O.R. 66n
judgements 83, 87, 88
justification 2, 62, 64, 79, 80, 91, 105

Kenny, Anthony 66n
know 40, 72
knowledge 4, 24, 27, 38, 42, 43, 68, 78, 85, 87, 92, 96, 98, 100, 101, 105, 111, 112
   of one's own mind 68
   of other minds 6, 95

language 1, 2, 5, 6, 34, 37, 38, 56, 57, 59, 60, 65, 66, 66n, 67n, 80, 86, 90, 102, 104, 105, 111
   initial 60, 67n1
   nature of 34
   new 60, 66n18
   ordinary 5, 34, 78
   protocol 37
   social nature of 65
   speaking of a 66
language game 36, 44, 45, 48, 49, 56, 57, 60, 78
learn 42
learning 41, 43
   of initial language 67n19
   of a new language 66n18
Locke, John 1, 72, 84, 92n, 97, 107
logical construction theory 73

Malcolm, Norman 90
Manser, Anthony 66n7
material object 76
materialistic monism 2
matter 1, 2
mean 1
meaning 46, 56, 62, 72, 89, 95
memory 6, 61, 63, 64, 65, 84, 85, 86, 87, 88, 89, 90, 91, 92, 94
   based statement 89, 90, 91
   criterion of personal identity 68
   statement 89, 90, 91
   theory of personal identity 107
mental 76, 77, 84
   acts 1, 3, 4, 7, 8, 71, 72, 76
   characteristics 12

Index

concepts 2, 3, 76, 78, 104
defect 13
events 5, 72
experience 7, 110
images 50, 61
phenomenon 7
processes 1, 7, 53
states 71, 72, 74, 75, 84, 100
Mill, J.S. 97
mind 1, 2, 3, 5, 6, 7, 19, 68, 70, 71, 72, 73, 74, 75, 76, 77, 78, 80, 81, 83, 95, 96, 97, 99, 102, 103, 104, 105, 106, 111, 112
   brain identity theory 7
   nature of 68, 71
Miri, Mrinal 86, 94n
Moore, G.E. 14, 66n
Müller-Lyer example 23, 24

name 61, 62, 76, 81, 102, 104
   of a sensation 56, 59, 60, 61
naming 53
   of a pain 52
neurophysiological process 7, 8
neurophysiology 28, 29
Newton 98
nonsense 48

observation 5, 11, 12, 16, 17, 18, 27, 32, 34, 74, 75, 78, 88, 97, 100, 105, 111
ordinary language analysis 112
organic sensations 9, 10, 11
organs of sense 9, 10, 77, 78
ostensive teaching 59
other minds 2, 6, 16, 25, 95, 96, 97, 98, 99, 100, 101, 102, 103, 104, 106, 109, 111
   problem of 96

pain 14, 15, 19, 39, 41, 42, 43, 44, 46, 47, 48, 50, 51, 52, 53, 54, 55, 56, 57, 58, 59, 60, 62, 66n, 71, 73, 74, 78, 80, 96, 99, 101, 102, 104, 105, 106
   behaviour 47, 58
   having a 14
Penelhum, T. 82
perception 8, 16, 18, 19, 21, 22, 24, 25, 28, 29, 30, 44, 73, 74, 93, 96, 110
   delusive 20, 21
   immediate 16, 29, 31

mediate 16
normal 21, 22, 24
objects of 16
veridical 20, 21
visual 16
perceptual phenomenon 20
perceive 13, 14
perceiving 12, 50
person 1, 69, 70, 73, 74, 76, 77, 79, 81, 82, 83, 84, 85, 86, 87, 92, 99, 100, 102, 103, 104, 107, 108, 109, 112
personal identity 6, 68, 82, 83, 84, 85, 86, 88, 95, 102, 104
phenomena 2
   psychical 6
philosophy 4, 16
physical 76, 77, 100
   object 15, 19, 20, 24, 27, 28
   reality 15, 16
   state 3
physiologist 7
physiology 28
Picasso 25
Plato 1, 70
Popper, Karl 103
Price, H.H. 14, 19, 20, 25, 26, 102, 103
primary concept 77
privacy 38, 46, 79, 106
   inalienability, sense of 38
   incommunicability sense of 38
private 16, 19, 38, 51, 53, 66, 95
   entities 5
   experiences 35, 37, 38
   sensations 35, 55
private language 2, 5, 6, 16, 34, 35, 36, 37, 38, 39, 52, 53, 61, 62, 63, 64, 65, 67n, 68, 79, 102, 106, 110
   notion of 34
   linguist 52, 53, 56, 60, 62
privileged access 68, 75, 79, 104, 110
problem of other minds 96
propositions
   law 76
   law like 76
protocol language 37
psychic 100
psychical process 1
psychological 3, 4, 41, 44, 45, 68, 78, 84, 100, 105, 107
   features 70
psychologist 14, 17
psychology 2, 7, 46

psycho-physical relationship 100, 101
public language 34, 35, 36, 37, 63
  object 59
pure-ego 70

Reid, Thomas 70, 71
remembering 61
retrospection 74, 75
Rip van Winkle 92
rules 34, 36, 37, 60, 62, 63, 65, 66n
  follow 63
  private 63, 66n
  semantic 36
  syntactic 36
Russell, B. 14, 19, 70, 73, 82, 84, 92n
Ryle, G. 3, 6, 7, 18, 32, 45, 68, 80, 81, 105, 110

same 50, 51, 62, 73, 87
sceptic 45, 49, 92, 99
scepticism 5, 7, 16
science 2, 3, 104
see 57
seeing 8, 22, 24, 25, 26, 29, 30, 57
self 68, 69, 71, 73, 81, 93, 103
  consciousness 83
  intimating 71
  knowledge 6, 68, 71, 74, 75, 81, 95, 102, 104
sensations 1, 5, 6, 9, 10, 11, 12, 13, 14, 15, 16, 17, 18, 32, 34, 35, 38, 39, 40, 42, 44, 46, 47, 48, 50, 51, 52, 53, 54, 55, 56, 57, 58, 59, 61, 64, 65, 66n, 68, 73, 95, 96, 100, 102, 103, 104, 110
  act of 11
  language 58
sense-data 5, 9, 14, 16, 18, 19, 20, 21, 22, 24, 25, 26, 27, 28, 29, 30, 31, 32, 34, 111
  datum 21, 24
  datum philosophers 18, 19, 20, 21, 26
  datum theory 18, 19, 32
  experience 19, 80

impressions 13, 14, 15, 16, 18, 19, 34
  organs 13, 14
  perception 19, 26, 32
  senses 19, 21
sensible qualities 5, 9, 13, 14
sensory experience 11
  illusion 21, 22
serial theory 73
Shoemaker, S. 7, 85, 90, 93n, 94n, 107, 108
siamese twins 49
sign 36, 61, 62, 64, 66n, 97
Smart, J.J.C. 3
soul 72, 106
speech acts 65
spiritual substance 72
Strawson, P.F. 82, 93n, 101
subjective justification 62
substance 70, 71, 72, 76, 83
  theory 73, 75

technical questions 29
technique 106
thinking 1, 2
third-person statements 69, 107
  identity judgements 88, 89, 95
  psychological statements 105
time lag 31, 75
  zones 54
Todd, W. 67n

use 89, 90

vicious circle 44

Wiggins, D. 85
Williams, B.A.O. 86, 94n, 109
Winch, P. 66n
Wittgenstein L. 3, 4, 5, 7, 35, 38, 44, 45, 47, 48, 49, 50, 51, 52, 53, 54, 55, 58, 59, 61, 62, 64, 65, 66n, 67n, 80, 81, 99, 103, 105
words 1, 2, 4, 6, 36, 37, 38, 48, 52, 53, 58, 60, 72, 76, 89, 90, 103
  number 53